Corruption and Corporate Governance in India

BY THE SAME AUTHOR

Human Rights and Terrorism in India

Ayodhya Ram Temple and Hindu Renaissance

Economic Development and Reforms in India and China

Hindus Under Siege: The Way Out

Sri Lanka in Crisis: India's Options

Terrorism in India: A Strategy of Deterrence for India's National Security

Rama Setu: Symbol of National Unity

Hindutva and National Renaissance

India's China Strategic Perspective

Virat Hindu Identity: Concept and its Power

Building the Sri Rama Temple in Ayodhya

The Ideology of India's Modern Right

2G Spectrum Scam

Corruption and Corporate Governance in India

Satyam, Spectrum and Sundaram

Subramanian Swamy, Ph.D. (Harvard)

Member of Parliament, India
Former Union Cabinet Minister for
Commerce, Law & Justice, India

HAR-ANAND
PUBLICATIONS PVT LTD

Reprint, 2026

Published by Ashok Gosain and Ashish Gosain for
HAR-ANAND PUBLICATIONS PVT LTD
E-49/3, Okhla Industrial Area, Phase-II, New Delhi-110020
Tel: 41603491
E-mail: info@haranandbooks.com/haranand@rediffmail.com
Shop online at: www.haranandbooks.com

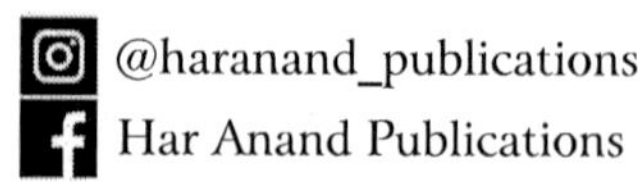

Printed in India at Megha Enterprises

Preface

The Satyam and Spectrum episodes have allowed us to look at the core of corporate governance in India: on whose behalf are public limited companies in India governed? Hence how can we reform governance rules to ensure the sustainability and effectiveness of the institution of corporate bodies, private and public in India? In his book *Supercapitalism* (Knopf 2007) former Clinton Cabinet member (Secretary of Labour), Dr. Robert Reich warns of the dangers of democracy being derailed if Supercapitalism, i.e., capitalism, that is globally-driven and web-based, is not governed by adequate regulation.

Sudhakar Ram, a CEO has recently articulated (*Economic Times,* March 16, 2009) some original ideas on this subject. In discussions on governance he points out that one question that does not get the attention it merits is: on whose behalf should a company be governed? Of course the conventional wisdom is that a company is governed on behalf of the shareholders.

The course of events at Satyam throws up enough doubts about this 'wisdom.' First, only a small percentage of those who held Satyam shares in November are shareholders today. Hence, the shareholders are the first to desert a sinking company. In fact among the various stakeholders of any company, the shareholders tend to be the least loyal—selling their holdings at the first sign of trouble. Hence it is most appropriate to view shareholders as suppliers of money and liquidity rather than as owners. Second, it is incorrect that government-appointed independent board protects the interests of shareholders, most of whom have bought shares at a throw-away price. In fact, a prominent independent Board member of Satyam was a Harvard Business School professor who is teaching the ethics of corporate governance to the students! Nothing else could have embarrassed HBS more!!

Is the company then governed on behalf of the employees? Protecting the jobs and interests of the 53,000 employees at Satyam was clearly one driver for the quick government intervention. Providing employment, however, cannot be the primary purpose of any organization. The company is definitely not governed on behalf of its employees. What about the customers? The need to continue servicing large international clients as well as protect India's IT reputation has played a role in the government's decision to act quick. Nevertheless, just as with employees, a company does not exist purely for the benefit of the customers. Then who? The composite stakeholder—a term encompassing the shareholders, customers, employees, suppliers and the society at large. The company ought to be *governed on behalf of all stakeholders.*

What is to be done if the interests of various stakeholders are in conflict? Moreover, there is a constant turnover of shareholders, employees, customers and suppliers since the nature of the company's business constantly changes—requiring new employees as well as servicing new customers. When the composition of stakeholders is constantly evolving, how does the Board actually decide the best interest of each of these stakeholders?

Govern the company for the company's own benefit. The settled law that the company is a distinct legal entity, independent of any shareholder or any other stakeholder, first was established by the House of Lords' famous judgment in *Solomon vs Solomon & Company* (1897). Hence the role of governance, then, ought to be stewarding of the company to achieve its full potential.

The answer to the question 'Whose company is it anyway' is therefore: No one's! A company thus is a unique and distinct individual with its own 'DNA' and destiny. The goal of corporate governance, according to Sudhakar Ram, thus is three-fold:

(i) Ensuring the long-term health and viability of the company;

(ii) Stewarding the company to fulfill its potential and to become as great as it can be; and

(iii) Adherence to the highest standards of ethics, statutory compliance and social responsibility.

In the case of Satyam, these goals were not attained because there was an undue concentration of power with the Founders which was disproportionate to their low shareholding. The Board moreover was far less 'independent' than required. Hence the core issue, clearly, is balance of power. While individual leadership is a key ingredient of success, visionary leaders know how to delegate and control a larger team, not just within the company but also in the form of independent board members and advisors, to distribute power and empower their companies to grow independent of themselves. They understand institutions can be built only if they become more important than their leaders.

The Board of the company is, in effect like the legislature, with the primary responsibility being to steward the company to achieve its full potential. While in theory, the Board is elected by the shareholders, its job goes beyond catering to only the shareholders. The Board balances the needs of the composite stakeholders: the shareholders, employees, customers, vendors and partners, and society at large.

The management of the company is like the executive branch, the arm of governance. Working under the broad policy of the Board, the management is accountable for meeting the objectives, within the ethics and values of the company laid down by the Board. Unfortunately, unlike in constitutional democracy today the role of the 'judiciary' is discharged by the Board itself on internal company issues, and by the regulatory bodies, and the courts when they relate to infringement of the laws of the land. The judicial role of the Board is, as Ram points out, not yet as well developed and is at the root of many corporate governance failures.

One possible remedy is to establish, empower and strengthen the company's corporate governance committee and ensure that its charter includes a systematic review of company performance on all fronts across stakeholders. Given the size and complexities of today's corporations, it will be worthwhile therefore to turn over this judicial role of the Board to some other statutory body under the Companies Act.

The corporate governance committee can also play the role of an 'independent press' by taking proactive approach in seeking stakeholders feedback, facilitated by external agencies, even whistleblower encouragement, and a reformed disclosure policy.

Hence, Spectrum and Satyam episodes allow us to look at the current state of corporate governance especially on whose behalf the company is to be governed, and how to devolve power for effectiveness of the institution of corporate bodies, so that Satyam and Spectrum lead to Sundaram in the corporate world.

The book is written with this objective in mind. This author has relied heavily on the existing literature in the field and contemporary accounts in popular writing on the Satyam and Spectrum frauds. Where possible I have acknowledged the writings of others. What is distinctive here in this study is the sharp focus I have tried to give to the underlying malfunctions in the governance that makes Satyams and Spectrums to happen.

SUBRAMANIAN SWAMY

CONTENTS

Chapter I

INTRODUCTION
THE PROBLEM OF CORRUPTION

There is a unanimous view throughout the world that corruption in any system will derail it. Corruption occurs when a certain party, unable to compete in a transaction on pure merit, uses its wealth or power to do so. Corruption is therefore inherently bad for the smooth functioning of any economic system. It blurs the incentive system because people are discouraged and disincentivised in using merit as a means to success.

Corruption misallocates resources from the meritorious to the unworthy, the immoral, the criminal, the powerful or the rich. Optimality conditions of trade for transactions thus are altered and transactions are effected sub-optimally. Moreover, since merit is regarded inferior to power, most transactions then lead to sub-optimal sub-standard goods and services, which could not otherwise have been sold openly. Thus, corrupt transactions result in the sale and purchase of goods or services of inferior quality, which is detrimental to the nation. Moreover, offices lose their legitimacy once they indulge in corruption, undermining people's trust in the political system along with the decline in the power of office to stem the rot of corruption. Colombia and Mexico are living examples of this. In the past flourishing empires have collapsed because of financial and moral corruption.

One of the worst problems with corruption in India is the creation of "black money," money that is used in such transactions is obviously unreported, and hence is neither taxed nor spent openly. It travels to secret bank accounts abroad, or worse, is used by the corrupt to indulge in gross luxurious consumption and bribery. While this in itself harms the country, it also has the effect of raising the profitability of non-essential and luxury industries, which in turn attract future investment to these industries. This crowds out investment in other, more essential industries. In India, the luxury goods sector, directly and indirectly receives 70% of the national investment. Black money also funds elections and hence there is no accounting. It tempts the receiver to stash and salt away part of the campaign funds. Since elections leads to political power of those funded, future governments become bribe-compliant and protect the crooked.

Corruption today is a popularly used word to mean to each citizen an act which he or she disapproves of. However, Transparency International has given a more concise but narrower definition: "Corruption is the misuse of public power for private profit."

Recent events have shown that this definition is not comprehensive. For example, match-fixing corruption in Cricket tournament is not a misuse of public power but of public expectation and trust. Therefore we re-define corruption here *as the misuse of any power of public consequence for private gain.*

Corruption is however an ancient problem. In a hoary treatise on public administration in India, the *Arthasastra,* Kautilya writes:

> "Just as it is impossible not to taste the honey (or the poison) that finds itself at the tip of the tongue, so it is impossible for a government servant not to eat up, at least, a bit of the king's revenue. Just as fish moving under water cannot possibly be found out either as drinking or not drinking water, so government servants employed in the government work cannot be found out (while) taking money (for themselves).

With characteristic precision, Kautilya states that there are "forty ways of embezzlement" and then goes on to enumerate them. Today, there must be 40,000 or more ways.

Therefore, the concept of corruption is being widened everyday. Under case laws laid down by the Supreme Court, it is corruption for example, when a former Union Minister of Environment, taking advantage of his official position, utilized large tracts of forest land in a hilly area to change its topography, and then divert the flow of the river in the valley below and all for commercial pelf—viz. establishing a Hotel Resort! Unfortunately for the former Minister, Justice Kuldip Singh, who was one of our senior environmentally vigilant Judges read an account of this in one of the national newspapers. In 1997, sitting as a Judge on the "Green Bench," he issued notice *suo moto* on all concerned authorities. After hearing the parties, the Supreme Court said that, the activities of the former Minister would constitute acts of environmental-degradation, and hence corruption.

The Court then invoked (for the first time) the *Doctrine of Public Trust* – holding that when a State holds a resource which is available for the free use of the public, Courts will look with considerable skepticism upon any governmental conduct which is calculated either to relocate that resource to more restricted uses or to subject public uses to the self-interest of private parties. When pronouncing judgment the Court said: "Our legal system is based on English Common law and includes the Public Trust doctrine as part of its jurisprudence" (1997 (1) SCC 388). Describing the Precautionary Principles and the Polluter Pays Principle as essential features of "sustainable development," the Court used the occasion to remind the Pollution Control Board of the State (of Himachal Pradesh) of its statutory obligations: not to permit the discharge of untreated effluent into the river Beas, and to inspect all hotels, institutions, factories in the entire area (of Kullu-Manali) and if in case any one of them was so discharging untreated effluent or waste into the river, the Court directed the Board to take action in accordance with law. He also directed payment of compensation for wrong done by the public official.

In a judgment handed down on February 1, 2000 (*State of M.P. v Ram Singh* — Judgment of Thomas J. and Sethi J. dt. 1/2/2000), two Judges of Supreme Court have likened the present state of corruption as akin to "a dreaded communicable disease" (like HIV) and they have said that socio-political system exposed to such a disease "is likely to crumble under its own weight." Words of dire warning if not of despair!

In 1966, the Administrative Reforms Committee, had recommended the institution of a Lokpal (Ombudsman). Pursuant to its recommendation the Lokpal Bill was introduced in the 4th Lok Sabha (1967-71). It was impolitely (but not inaptly) described by one journalist as "a rat trap for catching all kinds of rats—big and small." It was essentially intended to render speedy justice to citizens, but no one could be caught because the Bill could not be passed. After more than 25 years it is still not passed!

Public vigil against the corrupt however can be hampered by lawyers filing harassing defamation cases.

Defamation after all is an exception to the right to freedom of speech guaranteed by Article 19 (1) (a) of our Constitution. But these are times of openness and transparency, not only in this country but also all around the world. Hence we must leave the precious reputation of public figures to "market forces." Those who like to see their names and faces in the print and electronic media cannot be permitted to rush to court with defamation suits when some non-proven allegation is made against them; they are, after all, under public exposure, and must be subjected to the vagaries of the political market as are speculators, on the stock exchange. They also have access to the media, and can rebut the allegations. The greatest deterrent against combating corruption in public life, in my opinion, is the fundamental right of privacy for public persons, including officials. We will only be building a shield of armour for reputedly corrupt officials.

Justice Jeevan Reddy, as a Judge of the Indian Supreme Court, after hearing me before the First Bench with the CJI on the plethora of defamation cases filed against me by the Tamil Nadu Government, chose to adopt the ratio of the judgment of the U.S. Supreme Court in *New York Times vs Sullivan* [(1964) 376 US 254]: viz. that absent deliberate malicious intent on the part of the slanderer of public figures would not permit a complaint against unproven allegations of alleged wrong doings published in the media. His judgment in another case, the Gopal Nakeeran case [(1994) 6 SCC 306], has blazed a new trail in the law of defamation that gives greater protection to the publicly alert and vigilant to expose the corrupt without too much fear of harassment from defamation cases.

It is now evident that corruption has become a globalized phenomenon affecting more and more nations in the process. The stakes are also getting higher.

Transparency International (TI), a global civil society organization fighting corruption, recently released its 2008 Global Corruption Perceptions Index (CPI), measuring country-wise public-sector corruption levels through surveys in 180 countries. CPI for 2008 showed continuing high corruption levels in low-income countries and a slippage among wealthy countries. India has not come out with flying colours (see Table 1).

KPMG's *India Fraud Survey Report* 2008, which incorporated feedback from 1,000 organisations in India, also revealed that 28 per cent of respondents resorted to bribery either in a "business as usual" manner or "when faced with situations."

Box 1

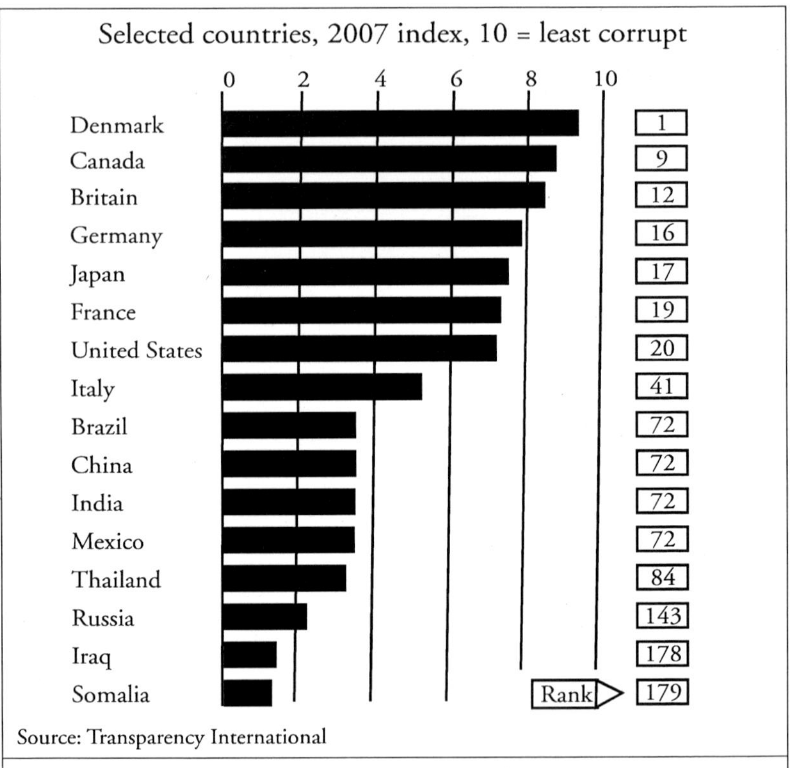

Source: Transparency International

PERCEPTIONS OF CORRUPTION

The poorest countries tend also to be the most corrupt, according to Transparency International. Its annual Corruption Perceptions Index is compiled from surveys of businessmen and country experts. This year's report brackets together New Zealand, Denmark and Finland as the least corrupt countries. Somalia and Myanmar suffer from the most corruption, defined as the abuse of public office for private gain. Conflict-ridden countries like Afghanistan, Iraq and Sudan also languish towards the bottom. Several African countries, including Namibia, the Seychelles, South Africa and Swaziland, improved their scores in the latest survey. But corruption is felt to have worsened in Austria, Bahrain, Jordan and Thailand.

Table 1
Transparency international's corruption index rankings indicate India is becoming a bit more corrupt; others show a mixed trend

	CPI* Rank		Score	
	2008	2007	2008	2007
Denmark	1	1	9.3	9.4
Singapore	4	4	9.2	9.3
Australia	9	11	8.7	8.6
Hong Kong	12	14	8.1	8.3
UK	16	12	7.7	8.4
Japan	18	17	7.3	7.5
US	18	20	7.3	7.2
France	23	19	6.9	7.3
South Korea	40	43	5.6	5.1
South Africa	54	43	4.9	5.1
Mexico	72	72	3.6	3.5
China	72	72	3.6	3.5
Brazil	80	72	3.5	3.5
India	85	72	3.4	3.5
Russia	147	143	2.1	2.3

*Corruption Perceptions Index of Transparency International (TI)
Ranks go from 1 to 180 with 1 being least corrupt and 180 most corrupt scores go from 1 to 10 with 1 being most corrupt and 10 being least corrupt.

TI's Chairperson Huguette Labelle in a recent press note stated: "The continuing high levels of corruption plaguing many of the world's societies amount to an ongoing humanitarian disaster." In the US, the 30-year old *Foreign Corruption Practices Act* (FCPA) lays out the rules and fines for attempts to bribe foreign government agents by American firms and their global subsidiaries. A KPMG US survey of 103 FCPA-compliance executives, however, shows that FCPA was more of a paper tiger. India got attention for the wrong reasons in this survey: 84 per cent strongly believed that Indian businesses pay bribes, euphemistically called facilitation payments. The recent Enron investigations under FCPA has brought this out clearly [see also Box 2].

Some US companies such as Dow Chemicals and Xerox, which have operations in India have actually faced action back home in US for FCPA violations. In February 2009, the US Department of Justice levied a $300,000 (Rs. 1.5 crore) penalty on Pioneer Friction, a wholly-owned subsidiary of US-based Westinghouse Air Brake Technologies (Wabtec) for bribing officials of the Indian Railway Regulatory Board. Pioneer, a brake blocks seller in the railway equipment market, made illegal cash payments, between 2001 and 2005—to the tune of $137,400—to Indian Railways officials to get their sealed bids in tender process approved and to maintain continued business operation. In the same case, the US Securities and Exchange Commission (SEC) settled with Wabtec for a disgorgement of profits of $288,000 and a penalty of $89,000.

In September 2007, SEC fined Chandramowli Srinivasan, President of AT Kearney, an Indian subsidiary of US-based Electronic Data Systems, for bribing senior officials of two semi-government energy companies—to get contracts and to prevent cancellation of existing contracts. The fine was about $720,000.

India needs to clean up its act to get rid of its image as a highly corrupt country. Corruption in some Indian states is more alarming than on the rest. A joint study in June 2008, by TI India and Centre for Media Studies on corruption in the country, showed Jammu and Kashmir, Madhya Pradesh and Uttar Pradesh as the "alarmingly" most corrupt States.

After most corrupt States in India, those figuring in the second rung as "very highly corrupt" States are Rajasthan, Karnataka and Tamil Nadu. Not as notorious, but still "highly corrupt" are the six States of Gujarat, Chhattisgarh, Delhi, Jharkhand, Kerala and Orissa. And on the rung as "moderately corrupt" are Maharashtra, Andhra Pradesh, Haryana, Punjab, Himachal Pradesh, West Bengal and Uttarakhand.

BOX 2

Department of Justice

FOR IMMEDIATE RELEASE
Thursday, January 8, 2009
WWW.USDOJ.GOV

CRM
(202) 514-2007
TDD (202) 514-1888

Former Executive at California Valve Company Pleads Guilty to Bribing Foreign Government Officials

WASHINGTON – A former executive of an Orange County, Calif.-based valve company pleaded guilty today in connection with his role in a conspiracy to pay approximately $1 million in bribes to numerous foreign government officials, Acting Assistant Attorney General Matthew Friedrich of the Criminal Division, U.S. Attorney Thomas P. O'Brien of the Central District of California and Joseph Persichini Jr., Assistant Director in Charge of the FBI's Washington Field Office announced.

Mario Covino, 44, an Italian citizen and resident of Irvine, Calif., pleaded guilty before U.S. District Judge James V. Selna in Santa Ana, Calif., to a one-count information charging him with conspiring to make corrupt payments to foreign government officials for the purpose of securing business for the Orange County valve company from state-owned enterprises in several countries, including Brazil, China, India, Korea, Malaysia and the United Arab Emirates (UAE), in violation of the Foreign Corrupt Practices Act (FCPA).

According to court documents, the valve company designed and manufactured service control valves for use in the nuclear, oil and gas, and power generation industries worldwide. Covino was the director of worldwide factory sales at the valve company from March 2003 through August 2007. In this position, Covino was responsible for overseeing new construction projects and the replacement of existing valves made by other companies and installed at customer plants in more than 30 countries.

In connection with his guilty plea, Covino admitted that from March 2003 through August 2007, he caused employees and agents of the valve company to make corrupt payments totaling approximately $1 million to foreign officials employed at state-owned enterprises in order to assist in obtaining and retaining business for the valve company. Covino also admitted that the valve company earned approximately $5 million in profits from the contracts it obtained as a result of these corrupt payments. According to the court documents, the corrupt payments were made to foreign officials at state-owned entities including, but not limited to, Petrobras (Brazil), Dingzhou Power (China), Datang Power (China), China Petroleum, China Resources Power, China National Offshore Oil Company, PetroChina, Maharashtra State Electricity Board (India), KHNP (Korea), Petronas (Malaysia), Dolphin Energy (UAE) and Abu Dhabi Company for Oil Operations (UAE).

Covino also admitted to providing false and misleading responses to internal auditors during a 2004 internal audit of the company's commission payments, and to deleting emails and instructing others to delete emails that referred to corrupt payments, for the purpose of obstructing the internal audit.

As part of his plea agreement, Covino has agreed to cooperate with the Department in its ongoing investigation. At sentencing, scheduled for July 20, 2009, Covino faces a maximum of five years in prison.

The case was prosecuted by Assistant Chief Hank Bond Walther and Trial Attorney Andrew Gentin of the Criminal Division's Fraud Section and Assistant U.S. Attorney Douglas McCormick of the U.S. Attorney's Office for the Central District of California. The case was investigated by the FBI's Washington Field Office.

The Transparency International (India) had randomly selected a sample of 22.728 BPL (Below Poverty Line i.e. the poorest) households from all across the country and they were surveyed to ascertain the extent of extortion. The Police Department in all these States topped the corruption ranking followed by the Forest Department, Land Records/Registration, and Housing. Electricity, banking, education, water supply and the National Rural Employment Guarantee Scheme fell under the other corrupt services.

The survey estimated that nearly Rs. 883 crore was paid as bribes in the year 2007 by BPL families to avail of these public services—which includes getting a ration card as well as for admission in schools. Of this bribe money, Rs. 214.8 crore was paid to the police.

South Asian corruption has two key characteristics that make it far more dangerous and damaging than corruption in other parts of the world.

1. Corruption occurs more severely at the top, not the bottom, thus distorting decisions on development programmes and priorities, and foisting sub-optimal choices on the people.

2. Corrupt money in South Asia has wings, not wheels, it thus is smuggled abroad to safe havens, not ploughed back and re-cycled into the domestic economy. It is like the Imperialist loot that bled India for centuries, and turned India from the richest to the poorest nation in two hundred years. (1750-1950).

In India, the year 1993 can be reckoned as a commencement year of mega corrupt events that set the trend for mega frauds in public life. That year, the JMM bribery scandal surfaced which unlike the Securities Scam did not involve the corruption of bureaucrats or police, but of Members of Parliament, causing a new low in India's democracy.

On 28th July 1993, ten MPs belonging to the Jharkhand Mukti Morcha and the Janata Dal cast their votes to defeat a no-confidence motion moved in the Lok Sabha against the minority government of Narasimha Rao. The CBI filed criminal cases against them saying that they were bribed to do so.

Since under Article 105 (2) of the Constitution of India no member of Parliament can be made liable to any proceedings in any Court in respect of any vote given by him in Parliament, the Supreme Court dismissed all cases against them: our "Founding Fathers" had not anticipated that fifty years down the road of parliamentary democracy there would be people's representatives themselves, selling their votes for monetary gain; and with impunity. This filthy exercise culminated in another No-Confidence Vote in Parliament in July 2008, when once again a Congress Government survived by these means. It is now seventeen long years after the Supreme Court verdict pleading constitutional helplessness but no new law or constitutional amendment has even been proposed.

The Prevention of Corruption Act (1988) provides for prosecution of public officials for corruption but it is bogged down by procedural provisions relating to mandatory prior permission and sanctions. Most important of all, there is no law for forfeiture of property acquired by corrupt means; such a Bill was framed by the Law Commission more than sixteen years ago but has not yet been introduced in Parliament.

Such anti-corruption laws as we have, grind slowly too slowly for the likes of the then Chief Vigilance Commissioner Vittal, who was an activist. He was applauded by some, though castigated by others, when he named 94 civil servants who were under investigation (accused of corruption on the basis of documentary evidence but not yet found guilty); their names were posted on the Internet on his instructions. "Sue me if you dare," Vittal had declared, but no one sued him! And it is now many years since Vittal retired. In 2003 the Central Vigilance Commission Act was passed by Parliament, constituting an independent Chief Vigilance Commission to supervise the Cental Bureau of Investigation. But as framed, it was and is only to catch "small-fish"; Central Government employees at the level of Joint Secretary and above have been made immune from any inquiry or investigation into any offence alleged to have been committed by them unless there is prior Central Government approval—which of course means political interference or protection for the "big-fish."

NGOs have sought to cater to popular sentiment against corruption by using "Sting Operations." When Tarun Tejpal of Tehelka fame was asked if it was legal to engage in an unlawful act like attempted bribery to trap someone suspected of being a bribe-taker, his response was: "I did not consult lawyers on the legalities, I was more bothered about the *monumental illegalities involved.*" He may have had a point: but allowing people to take law into their own hands undermines the rule of law. We need instead better laws and a less tolerant public.

What makes corruption most damaging to the nation is that money so made has "wings," and not wheels, because it is smuggled abroad to safe havens and out of easy reach. If faith in the administration of anti-corruption law is to be established, something drastic does need to be done. Reportedly, there are one and half trillion dollars stacked away by citizens of India in bank accounts in Switzerland. This does not include Cayman Island, the Isle of Man, Lichtenstein and other safe havens. Noted lawyer, Fali Nariman has suggested introducing a law nationalizing all Swiss Bank accounts held by Indian citizens, that permits exempting proven claims of genuine holders with legitimate credits. The onus to prove that would be on the holders. He suggested this to persons who matter in public life. But his suggestion has been received with an ominous silence. It is easy to speculate why. Too many skeletons will tumble out.

After the "group of twenty" meetings in London in early April, 2009, the Organisation for Economic Cooperation and Development (OECD) used "white-out" oil its blacklist of uncooperative tax havens made up of four countries: the Philippines, Malaysia, Costa Rica and Uruguay, these countries became willing to cooperate on illegal fund banking secrecy, and to make a disclosure.

But the OECD-which is made up of mostly European countries—also maintains a "grey" list, which includes its founding member Switzerland among a host of small island economies that are tax havens. Predictably, Switzerland has protested angrily.

According to the OECD, these tax havens—zero-tax jurisdictions that have no transparency and refuse to provide information to foreign tax authorities—enable individuals and companies to avoid the tax obligations of their home countries thereby depriving those governments of revenue that could go to building schools, hospitals and other public services. But it is the size of "lost" revenues that is starling estimates put the value of assets held in tax havens as much as $11.5 trillion!

Today there are more than 70 tax haven nations world-wide. Furthermore about forty countries openly advertise themselves as tax havens to woo depositors. Some have gone so far as to offer "perquisites" such as asylum or immunity to criminals, to those who invest sufficient funds. They permit the formation of companies without any proof of identity perhaps even by remote computer connections. Such extremes are however found in those emerging nations where the stability and security of the financial, legal, political systems are questionable.

The concessions and benefits may come in different forms. It may be a zero income tax for all (British Virgin Islands Business Companies), a complete tax exemption for all international business operated by non-residents (Seychelles or Belize

International Business Companies), an ultra-low income tax for international businesses (Seychelles Special License Companies, pay 1.5% tax), local tax exemption for non-residents of that jurisdiction (Gibraltar, Channel Islands); zero tax on receipt and distribution of dividends (holding companies in Cyprus, Denmark, Netherlands), tax holidays for certain types of investments (Portugal, Iceland); favorable tax treatment through treaties and agreements with the investor's home country (Cyprus, Netherlands, Malta), etc.

The Swiss Bankers Association (SBA), quoting Swiss National Bank figures, said the value of securities in custody accounts of the country's banks stood at 3.82 trillion Swiss francs (about US$ 3.35 trillion) in 2008. Founded in 1912, SBA has nearly 363 institutional members and about 16,000 individual members. Swiss National Bank, which is the nation's central bank, does not reveal the country-by-country breakdown of these figures, the SBA spokesperson said.

Of the total, securities held on behalf of foreign institutional, corporate and private clients touched more than 2.19 trillion Swiss francs (about US$ 1.92 trillion).

The Swiss Federal Department of Justice and police (FDJP) said in a report that the number of Suspicious Activity Reports (SARs) in connection with money laundering jumped from 795 in 2007 to 851 in 2008. This included nine related to suspected terror financing and involved assets worth over one million Swiss francs (US$ 884,600).

In 2008, the Money Laundering Reporting Office Switzerland (MROS) received 851 SARs, with nearly 67 per cent of them coming from the banking sector. Among them, most were related to investment fraud.

Finally, due to the US, the Swiss banking giant UBS, has been forced to disclose account details of clients, after admitting that it helped US Customers in tax evasion.

As the global crackdown gains momentum with cooperation from different countries, the world can hope of more and more money and valuable stashed away in tax havens to see the light of the day, sooner than later, thanks to the concern over terrorist funding globally.

In addition, some countries offer superior legal protection from creditors and potential litigants who might attempt to seize an individuals' wealth. This is the other most important reason why offshore jurisdictions are so popular—asset protection.

For those who face prosecution and imprisonment in their home country.

OECD suggests $11.5 trillion in all tax havens. In 2006, the most recent year of the Global Financial Integrity—[GFI] study, developing countries lost an estimated $858.6 billion to $1.06 trillion in illicit financial outflows.

Even at the lower end of the range of estimates, the volume of illicit financial flows coming out of developing countries increased at a compound rate of 18.2 per cent over the 5 year period analyzed for the study. On average, for the five-year period of this study, Asia accounts for approximately 50 per cent of overall illicit financial flows from all developing countries.

Financial flows in the context of this report includes the proceeds from both illicit activities such as corruption (bribery and embezzlement of national wealth, criminal activity, and the proceeds of licit business that become illicit when transported across borders in contravention of applicable laws and regulatory frameworks.

In the study illicit financial flows from developing countries: 2002-06 of the Global Financial Integrity [GFI], authors Dev Kar and Devan Castwright Smith estimate that the average amount stashed away from India annually during 2002-06 is $27.3 billion. This means that during the 5 year period, the amount stashed away was 27.3 x 5 = 136.5 billion. It is not as if that all these amounts had gone to Swiss banks but also has gone to different tax and secret shelters. Since the share of Swiss banks in dirty money is estimated at being a third of the global aggregate some $45 billion out of the 136.5 billion stashed away from India could have been hoarded in these years in Swiss banks. [p. 30 of the Report].

The important point is that this is only for 5 years. Therefore the loot of the previous 55 years would be several times that amount. Thus estimation is that the money from India stashed away abroad may be in the range of 1.5 trillion, an estimate suggested by L.K. Advani, and scoffed at by Congress Party intellectuals-in-residence.

The Interntional Narcotics Control Strategy Report—Money Laundering and Financial Crimes [March 2009 US Department of State] suggests that 30-40 per cent of the inflows may be by "Hawala" market. The report also suggests investigating NGO funding [nearly Rs. 65,000 crore from 1996 to 2006—Rs. 12700 crore in 2006-07 alone! Despite strict regulations pertaining to inflows on half of nearly 34,000 registered bodies submit details to Union Ministry of Home Affairs.

In the G-20 meet in April 2009, China forcefully argued for not disclosing the tax haven list since it worried that Hongkong and Macao would be listed. Hence, in the OECD list issued and noted by G-20, Hongkong and Macao were not included!

India did not argue at all against tax havens in the Meet or in the Preparatory Meet earlier. Obviously, Indian politicians worried that names of beneficiaries may come out!

One-third of the world's private fortune however is vested in banks in Switzerland in which country banking is a pillar of the economy—11 per cent of GDP in 2006 as against 5.8 per cent in 1990.

This opening came in stages from the time 18 years ago when Swiss banking authorities impounded and paid Phillipines about $624 million stolen by former President Marcos. Thereafter Switzerland joined a World bank and UN-led Global initiative to return money of corrupt politicians.

Thus in 2006 Nigeria got $700 million of former dictator Sani Abacha. Italy got it in 2002; Phillipines got it; Jews got it the Nazi loot in Swiss Banks. Then Peru recovered $180 millions deposited by Vladimiro Montesinos.

Financial Intelligence Unit-India (FIU-IND) has been admitted as the member of the Egmont Group as its recent Penary Session at Hamilton, Bermuda.

Membership of the Egmont Group, apart from meeting an important requirement of the Financial Action Task Force (FATF), will facilitate and enhance exchange of information by FIU-IND with its counterpart FIUs.

Unfortunately the Government does not reveal the nature and identification of Foreign Institutional Investors (FII) who are investing in the market nor the nature of origin of these entities. The Indian attitude to this serious issues is a contrast to how the US handles it. For instance, the UBS paid a penalty of over $800 millions in US recently and also disclosed the secret account details of nearly 300 Americans to the US government.

But in India the same UBS paid a paltry penalty a Rs. 55 lakhs to the SEBI for not—yes for NOT—disclosing the names of the secret PN holders whose funds it had invested, and settled the case, a month back!

The PN is the mechanism through which unnamed investors are allowed to participate in the stock market.

The G-20 Summit the communiqué issued on 2 April 2009, in paragraph 15, entitled, "Strengthening the Financial System," pledged themselves "to take action against non-cooperative jurisdictions, including tax havens. We stand ready to deploy sanctions to protect our public finances and financial systems. The era of banking secrecy is over. We note that the OECD has today published a list of countries assessed by the Global Forum against the international standard for exchange of tax information?"

"Overview of the OECD's Work on International Tax Evasion," the OECD lists studies that state that between $1.7 trillion to $11.5 trillion from 185 UN member countries are today parked in the 70 tax havens of the globe. Hence, the e-mail circulated estimate for India at $1.5 trillion attributed to the Swiss Bank Association has been officially denied by the Association as "fabricated." In a sarcastic comment, the Association spokes persons said the issue has become "good election fodder" and that the amounts being mentioned were "quite incredible." "I just don't know the methodology on how they arrived at the figures, the Association spokesman James Nason said. The basic point however is: even if the amounts are just tens of billion dollars, and not one and a half trillion dollars, they should be brought back to India. And the fact is that other countries, much smaller countries with none of the pretensions of being a "super power, have already succeeded in getting their money back. Since October 2008, when the OECD released its paper, several countries have succeeded in recovering billions of dollars.

ILLEGAL OUTFLOW

In $billion

China	22,289
Saudi Arabia	54-55
Mexico	41-46
Russia	32-38
India	23-27

Figures are annual illicit financial flows from development countries for 2002-06 period. *Source:* GFI, Washington DC 2008. Total capital flight from developing countries-$1 trillion per year.

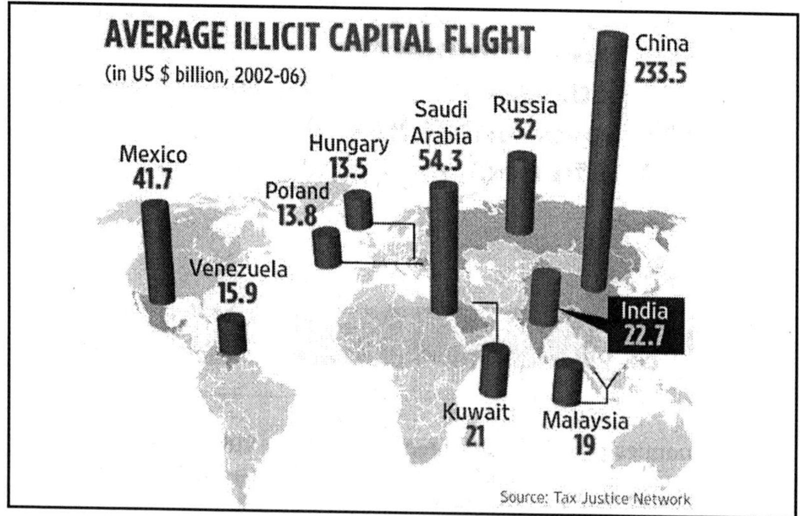

But the UPA government instead had allowed Ottavio Quattrochi to take his money out of banks—where it was lying frozen on court orders. Thus, such a Government which castrated the CBI to let him get away from Argentina with the loot cannot be trusted to bring the billions of dollars stashed away in tax havens. It needs a decisive new government.

However for five reasons why it's not going to be easy: even for a new government:

- India needs to have tax/fund information sharing as part of bilateral agreements with tax havens.
- Also needs supporting agreements to repatriate funds of suspected felons. This would of course take grit.
- Some Tax havens also need to relax their banking secrecy rules.
- India would have to furnish names of suspected fraudsters and establish illegality of bank account holder's fund source or quote a law passed by parliament.
- Fraud component in each individual case will need to be proved, which is a lengthy process. "Fishing" will not work.

The Swiss Ambassador to India, Dreyer addressing a press conference in 2007 to commemorate the 60 years of Indo-Swiss Friendship Treaty had said: "Switzerland was accused of giving shelter to black money and there has been a lot of inflow of such wealth from India and other countries of the world. He added: "I would not say it would be stopped 100 per cent (under a new law). But through this measure, it would be controlled up to a certain limit." [On 15-03-2008 in NDTV Profit]. He was referring to an agreement that Switzerland had signed with the World Bank and the UN-led global initiative to money deposited by corrupt persons in Swiss banks, and the confisacation and return of the money to their country of origin.

The Lichtenstein tax haven came into focus recently Germany's intelligence agency paid an unnamed informer more than USD 6 million for confidential and secret data about clients of LGT group a bank owned by the Liechtenstein royalty.

The revelations therefrom have already led to the resignation of the head of Deutsche Post—the former German mail service—which is currently the world's largest logistics company in the world. The Lichtenstein leaders are furious and have focused all their ire at the theft of the data rather than on the facts of the case.

The German Government has also announced that it would share information on accounts held in the tax haven with any Government that wanted it. They had a list of 1400 clients of whom 600 only Germans. The spokesman for the German Finance ministry Thorstein Albig has indicated that they would respondent to such request without charging any fees for the information. Finland, Sweden and Norway have expressed interest in the data obtained by the Berlin intelligent agency.

Even where foreign governments offer to help, the Indian government has fought shy of availing the offer. In May 2008, the German Government offered to share information relating to illegal Indian bank accounts in Liechstein, which information had tumbled out while Germany was investigating their own citizens' accounts. Despite Prime Minister Dr. Manmohan Singh's personal assurance to me in writing (see p. 26), nothing to date has been done despite pious noises of the Government.

The prospects of combating corruption are thus very grim. Is there a solution?

The Frenchman Jean Monet who conceived the idea of a European Union way back in 1948, often used to say that there are two types of people in this world. Those who do something and those who want to keep *talking about doing something.* Even with present laws, there is much that can be done to fight corruption if only there is a national resolve and cultural value inculcated for the same.

The Prevention of Corruption Act (1988) even in the present form is sufficient to initiate action and bring public odium to the corrupt public officials. To prosecute a State Minister for corruption, the sanction of the State Government is of course required, which effectively means the sanction of the Council of Ministers. Corruption amongst State Minister is, therefore, as controlled or as endemic as the State's Chief Minister for the time being, chooses to tolerate! The same caveat holds for the Union Ministers too as we saw recently in the Mr. Laloo, Ms. Mayawati and Mr. Mulayam Singh Yadav cases. Chief Ministers remained—till recently— immune from prosecution since there was doubt about the "Appointing Authority" to give sanctions. It was Air Chief Marshall Latif (appointed Governor by the then Union Government) who brought laurels to that high office when in 1982 he granted sanction to prosecute Maharashtra's then Chief Minister (who also belonged to the Congress party). In 1995, Tamil Nadu Governor Dr. Chenna Reddy also dared to give sanction to me to prosecute the then Chief Minister. All this was

Your Saturday Newspaper

NIE, Chennai, 10/5/08 Rupees 1.50 | pages 38 | Late City Edition

IN ONE OF THE BIGGEST BLACK MONEY SCANDALS EVER, GERMAN INTELLIGENCE HAS A LIST OF ACCOUNTS AT A LIECHTENSTEIN BANK. GERMANY SAYS IT WILL GIVE THE LIST TO ANY GOVERNMENT THAT ASKS. THREE MONTHS HAVE PASSED, BUT INDIA STILL HASN'T ASKED

INDIA SILENT ON GERMAN BANK DISCLOSURE OFFER

Deutsche Post CEO Klaus Zumwinkel, whose arrest on February 14 broke open the LTG bank scandal.

Well-known tax havens

Andorra, Anguilla, Antigua & Barbuda, Antilles (Netherlands), Aruba, Bahamas, Barbados, Belize, Bermuda, British Virgin Islands, Campione d' Italia, Canary Islands, Cayman Islands, China, Cook Islands, Costa Rica, Cyprus, Dominica, Dominican Republic, Gibraltar, Guernsey, Island of Mauritius, Jersey, Isle of Man, Latvia, Liechtenstein, Luxembourg, Madeira, Mauritius, Nauru, Nevis, Niue, Malta, Panama, Switzerland, Turks & Caicos Islands, Western Samoa

Aditya Sinha
Chennai, May 9

NEARLY three months ago, Germany obtained a list of account holders at a bank in Liechtenstein, a tiny Alpine principality that is also a tax haven. The Germans offered the names to any country that asked for it. Curiously, India, with a history of black money stashed abroad, has shown no interest in the list; it still has not made a request for details.

On February 14, Deutsche Post CEO Klaus Zumwinkel was arrested in Berlin for tax evasion. His name was on a DVD that BND, Germany's intelligence agency, bought from a former bank employee of the LTG Group, run by Liechtenstein's ruling dynasty.

The disc had the names of 1,400 account holders of the LTG Group's Treuhand subsidiary. BND bought the list, dating from 2002, for Euros 4.2 million. Six hundred of the names lived in Germany, with a possible tax evasion of around Euros 5 billion; Berlin launched 125 tax investigations.

On February 25, German finance ministry spokesman Thorsten Albig announced that the names and details of the other 800 account holders would be given to their respective countries, at no extra cost.

ONLY IN EXPRESS

All the countries had to do was ask for them.

Finland, Norway and Sweden promptly asked. The USA, Australia, France, UK, Ireland, Italy, Canada, New Zealand and Spain subsequently put in requests. The Americans are now investigating 100 potential tax evaders on that list. Independently, the British stumbled onto information on 400 Italians with accounts at a Liechtenstein bank, and leaked it to the media.

India, however, which has long tried to uncover details of bank accounts in Switzerland and St Kitts, has not made a request. It should be made by the finance ministry through the ministry of external affairs, for it is something that concerns the Central Board of Direct Taxes, the Directorate of Enforcement and the Central Bureau of Investigation. Though the government is aware of the developments in Germany, till date, no request has gone, informed sources told *Express*.

Incidentally, Liechtenstein's Prince Hans-Adams II, the owner of the LTG group, has visited India, to a warm welcome by our political class.

adityasinha@epmltd.com

Hidden money, worldwide

UK-based Tax Justice Network's *The Price of Offshore* (2005) estimated how much wealth has been stashed away in tax havens worldwide by rich individuals. Remember: $1 trillion = $1,000 billion = Rs 4,00,000 crore

$11.5 trillion personal wealth was held off-shore by rich individuals, in about **70** tax havens worldwide

Interest earned **$860 billion** per year from their assets

Tax lost every year **$255 billion**

Offshore estimates by Boston Consulting Group

BCG, in its *Global Wealth Report for 2003*, was more conservative in its estimates

- Estimated total wealth of high net-worth individuals (HNWIs) at $38 trillion
- Of that, $9 trillion was held offshore

Middle East and Asia **$4.1 trillion** was kept offshore out of **$10.2 trillion** total HNWI wealth

Dr. Subramanian Swamy Ph.D. (Harvard)
President, Janata Party
Minister for Commerce, Law & Justice (1990-91)
Chairman (with Cabinet rank), Commission on Labour Standards and International Trade (1994-96)
Member of Parliament (1974-99)
Professor of Economics, Indian Institute of Technology, Delhi (1969-91)
Faculty, Harvard University (1963-69, 1985-86, 2001-08 Summer)

JANATA PARTY
A-77, Nizamuddin (East) New Delhi - 110 013, India
Phone : +91 24353805 Fax : +91 24357388
Mobile : +91 9810194279 ; +91 9940203333
Website : www.janataparty.org; www.indiaright.org
E-mail : swamy@post.harvard.edu
swamy39@gmail.com

May 11, 2008

Dr. Manmohan Singh,
Prime Minister of India,
New Delhi.

Dear Prime Minister,

Enclosed is a news paper cutting from May 10, 2008 edition of the New Indian Express, Chennai, which discloses that data on secret bank accounts in Liechenstein have come into the possession of the German government, which data the said Government is prepared to give to any other government making a formal request for the same.

I have verified from German official sources that the said NIE report is accurate on reporting of material facts.

Kindly therefore direct your officials to obtain these data records from Germany, and make them public by posting it as the PMO's website.

I had already written last year to you that the UN Secretary General's office has the chits issued by the erstwhile Saddam Hussein Iraqi government in favour of certain Indian politicians in the Oil for Food Programme and also that UN officials had told me at their New York Headquarters that they will supply the same to your Government if you put in a formal request. This you have not done yet.

Hence If you do not direct your office to get these records by June 15, 2008, I shall approach the Courts to enforce the performance of your statutory duty as Prime Minister in this regard.

Since you have been stating recently on the need to combat corruption I am encouraged to think that you will act in this matter.

I have known you for 40 years as a man of personal integrity and honesty. Therefore I expect that when it comes to matters of corruption especially when there is a paper trail you will act, especially since the PM's chair symbolizes the sovereignty of India, which you must defend, without fear or favour.

With Personal Regards,

Yours sincerely,

(SUBRAMANIAN SWAMY)

Encl. a/a

प्रधान मंत्री
Prime Minister

New Delhi
28 May, 2008

Dear Dr Swamy,

Thank you for your letter of May 11 enclosing a cutting from the Chennai-based New Indian Express.

We were aware that the German Government is investigating secret bank accounts in Liechtenstein. Appropriate action has already been taken by our Ministry of Finance, who are in contact with the German authorities in this connection. You need not, hence, have any apprehension that the Government is dragging its feet in this matter.

With regards

Yours sincerely,

Manmohan Singh
(Manmohan Singh)

Dr. Subramanian Swamy
Janata Party
A-77, Nizamuddin (East)
New Delhi-110 013

the result of a judicially innovated expedient—devised and sanctioned *not by elected representatives of the people,* but by non-elected Judges. A Chief Minister guilty of corruption could never be prosecuted since there was no statutory "appointing authority" to sanction his prosecution as required under the Act. In Chief Minister Antulay's case, the Court laid down that sanction would be given—of necessity—by the Head of State, the Governor, who in this matter (and in this matter alone) *would have to act in his own individual discretion, and not with the aid and advice of his Council of Ministers as* otherwise generally under Article 161 of the Constitution.

More heartening has been the response of our presently constituted Supreme Court in a case from Madhya Pradesh. Two ministers of the BJP-led State Government were, after investigation, indicted by the Lok Ayukta, who, in 1997, submitted a Report in 1997 to the Assembly that there were sufficient grounds for prosecuting them under the Prevention of Corruption Act (1988). Sanction was applied for from the Council of Ministers for prosecuting the two ministers. But the then Council of Ministers—with the Chief Minister at its head—refused Sanction on the ground that no *prima facie* case was made out! The papers were then submitted to the Governor for his signature approving of the Council of Ministers' recommendation.

Under the Constitution the Governor was bound by the advice of his Council of Ministers (Article 161). But the then Governor (Dr. Bhai Mahavir) went through the available documents and noted that the documentary evidence was more than sufficient to establish a *prima facie* case for prosecution. Despite the unanimous decision of the Council of Ministers, in November 1998 the Governor granted sanction for prosecution under Section 197 of the Criminal Procedure Code: His action was challenged in the High Court where unfortunately the challenge was upheld, and the

Sanction quashed. But the Supreme Court on an Appeal in a Constitutional Bench decision of five Judges (in November 2004) overturned the verdict.

Relying on the Report of the Lok Ayukta (and there again full marks for the institution of Lok Ayukta since the particular Lok Ayukta was able to act despite the wishes of the Party in power in the State), the Supreme Court declared the decision of the Council of Ministers as null and void, since in exonerating two of themselves they were acting as Judges in their own cause, which in law was impermissible. Justice had triumphed.

This case highlights two things viz. *first,* the importance in our constitutional scheme of the role of a Governor that he is and should be the conscience-keeper of the people of the State. *Second,* the importance of the role of Judges of the Supreme Court of India in boldly setting their face against the tidal wave of bribery and corruption that is engulfing us. It is a sorry reflection on our system of Parliamentary democracy [i.e. government by the people (through its elected representatives) for, and in the interests of the people] that these high functionaries invariably fail to act. But thanks to the checks and balances in our Constitution, there is still hope of doing something about corruption.

In another judgment of the Supreme Court delivered by Justice Jeevan Reddy in 1996, the Court had recommended that there was a crying necessity in the present state of our society that we should enact a law providing for forfeiture of properties acquired by holders of public office including offices and posts in the public sector corporations, where such properties had been acquired by indulging in corruption and illegal acts.

Once it was proved that the holder of such office had indulged in corrupt acts, (the Court said) all such properties should be attached forthwith. The law should place the burden of proving that the attached properties were not acquired with monies and properties received in the course of corrupt deals entered into by the holder of these properties. "Such law," said the Court, "is an absolute necessity if the canker of corruption is not to prove the death knell of this nation." When the Judge retired, he was appointed Chairman of the Law Commission of India. He himself then drafted and handed over to the Government of the day, the Corrupt Public Servants (Forfeiture of Property) Bill. It had only to be introduced in both Houses of Parliament where it would have been passed. Ten years have elapsed since then—and neither the previous Government nor the present Government—both "popular" governments—have thought it fit even to present the Bill in Parliament.

What can one or more individuals do against this tidal-wave of corruption? The Editor, *Nouvelle Revue Francoise,* a journal in France has provided an answer long ago. He was its Editor until he was ousted by his own kinsmen who had collaborated with the invading Nazi German army in 1942. He then joined the "Resistance," and when asked what could one Frenchman do against such heavy odds, his answer was: "You can squeeze a bee in your hand until it suffocates but it would suffocate after stinging you—that's precious little, you will say, but if it did not sting you, bees would have become extinct a long time ago."

Thus, if India expects to be considered a world power, it will have to take steps to minimize corruption, to bring the nation to the level of the five cleanest countries.

Corruption is a challenge not only for public officials but even in implementing economic reforms in a globalized framework. Although there is much open discussion in the last decade, and despite the global anti-corruption and awareness-raising campaign, corruption has not declined worldwide.

However, corruption as we find now is however not unique to developing countries, nor has it declined on average globally. In fact, some developing countries, such as Chile and Botswana do exhibit lower levels of corruption than some fully industrialized nations. Countries like Colombia and Liberia have made gains in combating corruption in recent years, while others, such as Zimbabwe, have deteriorated. Bribery remains rife in many countries, totaling about $1 trillion globally every year. It is not anymore just petty palm greasing for speedier file movement on the bureaucrat's table. We are now in a world of billion dollar Ponzi schemes and political patronage for the same.

The cost to society of bribing a bureaucrat to obtain a permit to operate a small firm, pales in comparison with, say, a telecommunications conglomerate that corrupts a politician to shape the rules of the game granting it monopolistic rights, or an investment bank influencing the regulatory and oversight regime governing them.

Hence, as a country becomes industrialized, its governance and corruption challenges do not disappear. They simply morph and become more sophisticated: It becomes a far more complex phenomenon than merely the transfer of a briefcase stacked with cash.

Instead, now, subtler forms of "legal corruption" exist e.g., an expectation of a future job for a regulator in a lobbying firm, or a campaign contribution with strings attached. In many countries this may be legal, even if unethical. In industrialized nations, undue influence is often legally exercised by powerful private interests, which in turn influence the nation's regulations, policies and laws. This has dire consequences: witnessed in the various forms of corruption underlying the current global financial crisis that started in the U.S. Concrete examples abound as given below:

First, two corporations, Freddie Mac and Fannie Mae spent millions of dollars lobbying some influential members of Congress in exchange for (among other things), lowering capital reserve requirements for these mortgage giants.

Second, AIG's derivatives unit located in London managed to fudge its accounts helped by lax regulatory oversight, and took wild risks that brought down AIG's empire of 100,000 employees in 130 countries, thus catalyzing the global financial crisis.

Third, giant mortgage lenders such as Countrywide Financial were permitted to switch regulators, so as to fall under the lax oversight of the Office of Thrift Supervision [paid for by the regulated banks and in turn which also supervised AIG's derivative unit!]

Fourth, During a G-5 meeting at the Securities and Exchange Commission in April 2004 the largest investment banks persuaded the SEC to relax its regulatory oversight and allow a much larger amount of debt than was provided for in the norm.

Finally, Madoff's giant Ponzi scheme, points to subtler forms of corruption. The SEC knew that Madoff, (who had served on the commission's own advisory committee), was then misleading it in how he managed the funds of his customers. Yet the SEC failed in detecting the Ponzi scheme till billions of dollars were lost.

Therefore corruption ought to include acts that may be legal in a strict narrow sense but where the rules of the game have been bent or permitted to utilise "scorched earth" techniques. Would this broader view of corruption result in a different corruption rating of nations? There is no doubt about that.

For example, over the past few years, traditional measures of corruption, such as the Corruption Perceptions Index of Transparency International, place the U.S. among the least corrupt nations in the world, (currently ranking No. 18 among 180 rated countries). In 2004 Dr. Daniel Kaufman of Brookings Institution, Washington D.C. had calculated an index of "legally corrupt" manifestations (measured through the extent of undue influence through political finance and powerful firms influencing politicians and policy making) and found that the U.S. rated in the bottom half among the 104 countries surveyed! The U.S. was rated 53rd, a few ranks below Italy. Netherlands, Norway, Denmark and Finland exhibited low levels of "legal corruption" (ranking Nos. 1 through 4, respectively). Chile was rated 18th. Also rating better than the U.S. were countries like Botswana, Colombia and South Africa!!

This is happening along with the new expanding role of government. But in order to restore confidence, citizens, entrepreneurs and bankers need to have renewed trust in the financial system. Transparency is therefore the key.

In this context, the World Bank in which nations are represented as members in the governing body, had decided to make public the names of all companies that have been debarred from receiving direct contracts from the Bank Group under its corporate procurement program. This change was made in the interest of fairness and transparency and aligns with the disclosure practice for companies that provide goods and services directly to the Bank with the current policy governing procurement on Bank financed projects in developing countries. In parallel with the Bank's disclosure of the names of companies and individuals debarred on Bank financed projects from now on, the Bank Group will publicly list the names of companies debarred from its corporate procurement for "palm greasing" and other corrupt practices.

A complete list of the 111 companies and individuals currently debarred from participating in Bank financed projects are available in www.worldbank.org. It shows that UK leads the list with 37 companies, while India has now entered this list with 3 companies.

There are currently three companies that have been debarred along with their affiliates under the Bank Group's corporate procurement program.

These black-listed Indian firms are:

1. Satyam Computer Services, Ltd.
   Term: 8 years
   Date: September 2008
   Reason: Providing improper benefits to Bank staff and failing to maintain documentation to support fees charged for its subcontractors.
2. Wipro Technologies
   Term: 4 years
   Date: June 2007
   Reason: Providing improper benefits to Bank staff
3. Megasoft Consultants Ltd.
   Term: 4 years
   Date: Dec 2007
   Reason: Participating in a joint venture with Bank staff while also conducting business with the Bank

US' INFAMOUS FRAUDS THAT SHOOK THE GLOBAL ECONOMY

General Motors (i.e. GM)

GM accelerated the booking of income from 2002 to 2006. It did this by improperly accounting for supplier credits, cash flows and two one-time transactions based on product recalls.

The car-maker also failed to disclose legacy benefits to former GM workers, who left in 1999 to become employees of Delphi Corp., an auto parts company that was spun off from GM that year.

After being sent to mediation, GM agreed to pay $277 million.

Accountants

Deloitte and Touche, which served as independent auditor for the auto company, was accused of falsely certifying that GM's financials adhered to GAAP. Deloitte agreed to foot an additional $26 million to settle the charges.

Enron

Enron delivered smoothly growing earnings (but not cash flows). Wall Street took Enron on its word but didn't understand its financial statements. It was all about the price of the stock. In its last 5 years, Enron reported 20 straight quarters of increasing income. Enron, that had once made its money from hard assets like pipelines, generated more than 80% of its earnings from a more vague business known as "wholesale energy operations and services." The company avoided hundreds of millions of dollars in taxes by its use of stock options. Corporate executives received large quantities of stock options. When they exercised these options, the company claimed compensation settlement in the case, agreeing to pay $24.75 million out of their own pockets. Insurance covered the rest.

Accountants

A lawyer for a group of WorldCom Inc stockholders and bondholders had said former auditor Arthur Anderson LLP, (who was caught in the middle of thss auditing scandal too) was more concerned with "lining its own pockets" than catching a massive accounting fraud at the telecommunications company. Instead of asking tough questions of WorldCom's top executives or continuing to demand access to company records, Arthur Anderson shrugged its shoulders and acquiesced with a client that paid the firm more than $40 million in auditing and consulting fees in a three-year span.

Xerox

In the latest scandal involving a prominent American corporation, Xerox revealed in 2002 that over the past five years it has improperly classified over $6 billion in revenue, leading to an overstatement of earnings by nearly $2 billion. The effect of the manipulation was that Xerox could count as earnings what essentially was future revenue.

This boosted short-term profits and allowed the company to meet profit expectations in 1997, 1998 and 1999, though it had the effect of reducing earnings during the past two years. In 1998, Xerox reported a pretax income of $579 million, while it should have reported a loss of $13 million. On the other hand, the $137 million loss for 2001 will become a $365 million gain after the manipulation expense on their tax returns. Accounting rules let them omit that same expense from the earnings statement. The options only needed to be disclosed in a footnote. Options allowed them to pay less tax and report higher earnings while, at the same time, motivating them to manipulate earnings and stock price.

Accountants

Arthur Anderson LLP, which was one of the big 5, was convicted of obstruction of justice for shredding documents related to its audit of Enron, resulting in the Enron scandal. Nancy Temple (Andersen legal department) and David Duncan (lead partner for the Enron account) were cited as the responsible managers in this scandal, as they had given the order to shred relevant documents. Since the US Securities and Exchange Commission does not allow convicted felons to audit public companies, the firm agreed to surrender its CPA licenses and its right to practice before the SEC on August 31, 2002 - effectively putting the firm out of business in the US. Meanwhile, Arthur Anderson's non-US practice ceased to be viable due to reputational collateral damage. Most of them were taken over by local firms of other major international accounting firms.

WorldCom

WorldCom, US's second largest long distance telecommunications company, announced that it had overstated earnings in 2001 and the first quarter of 2002 by more than $3.8 billion. The accounting maneuver responsible for the overstatement was classifying payments for using other companies communications networks as capital expenditures. WorldCom filed for the reversed of the above practice. The $1.9 billion total that will now be subtracted from revenue reported from 1997-2001 will be added to future reports. Xerox has not been accused of falsely creating unearned income. Rather, it spread its income out in a fraudulent manner. To the same end, WorldCom improperly capitalised about $4 billion in ordinary expenses in order to allow the company to deduct the expense over a period of decades rather than writing it off all at once. Both these methods serve to boost short-term profits.

Accountants

The SEC settled its securities fraud case related to improper accounting at Xerox with the four remaining defendants, all of who were partners at the company's outside auditor at the time, KPMG. The four are: Ronald Safran, engagement partner on the Xerox audit for 1998 and 1999; Michael Conway, senior engagement partner for 2000; Anthony Dolanski, engagement partner for 1997; and Thomas Yoho, the SEC concurring review partner for KPMG on the Xerox engagement from 1997-2000. Safran, Conway, and Dolanski agreed to the entry of an injunction, with Safran and Conway paying civil penalties of $150,000 and Dolanski paying a $100,000 penalty. Yoho settled a separate administrative proceeding brought by the Commission and was censured. According to the SEC's Litigation Release, the audit fraud allowed Xerox to manipulate its earnings by over a billion dollars during the relevant period. The settled SEC order against

Yoho finds that he engaged in improper professional conduct by failing to exercise appropriate due care and professional skepticism when he conducted an "indepth" review during the 2000 audit. The company field for bankruptcy protection on July 21, 2002. On August 8, the company announced that it had also manipulated its reserve accounts in recent years, affecting an additional $3.8 billion. They admitted that the company had classified over $3.8 billion in payments for lines costs as capital expenditures rather than current expenses. Line costs are what WorldCom pays other companies for using their communications networks; they consist principally of access fees and transport charges for messages for WorldCom customers. Reportedly, $3.055 billion was misclassified in 2001 and $797 million in the first quarter of 2002. According to the company, another $14.7 billion in 2001 line costs was treated as a current expense. By transferring part of a current expense to a capital account, WorldCom increased both its net income (since expenses were understated) and its assets (since capitalised costs are treated as an investment). Had it not been detected, the maneuver would have resulted in lower net income in subsequent years, as the capitalised asset was depreciated.

Essentially, capitalising line costs would have enabled the company to spread its current expenses into the future, perhaps for 10 years or even longer. WorldCom also announced that it was also investigating possible irregularities in its reserves accounts. Companies establish these accounts to provide a cushion for predictable events, such as future tax liabilities, but they are not supposed to manipulate them to change reported earnings. On August 8, WorldCom admitted that it had improperly used its reserves in recent years. The indictments issued August 28 charged that reserve accounts were reduced in order to provide credits against line expenses. WorldCom's 12 outside directors have agreed to a $60.75 million fine.

With such spreading corrupting, are freedom and market systems the facilitators of such fraud and corruption? Is there any value to focusing on individual cases of corruption however big rather than on the systemic basis for such corruption?

The answer is that focusing on both is necessary. A simple mathematical analysis based on probability of detection, the cost to the corrupt of such detection, averaged by the expected value of the gain from the corrupt act, proves that even if the probability of detection is low (as generally it is), if the cost of detection to the corrupt is some multiple of the gain from the corrupt act then no rational person would choose to bribe or to accept a bribe. This is because the expected value of any corrupt transaction then becomes negative.* Hence, focusing on individual cases and making an example of them is useful for fighting corruption.

If thus Indian society is able to make an example of the two most glaring cases of corruption—Satyam and Spectrum, then the nation can look forward to becoming "Sundaram" again, because then no one will find any incentive to be corrupt even if the probability of being caught is small.

On the question of systemic basis of corruption, namely the Leftist view that freedom and competitive market are more prone to corruption, the world has come around to the view that a healthy democracy is essential for full human development, which however can be nurtured only through education and skill development. Democracy cannot be sustained unless the electorate is intellectually empowered by informed intelligence, a multi-dimensional concept, to make everyday moral judgments over

*If B is the value of a bribe enjoyed if not caught, and D is penalty suffered if caught, a minus, then assuming 'P' is the probability of being caught, the expected value of a corrupt transaction is $E(X) = PD + (1 - P)B$. If D is assumed to be multiple of B, i.e., $|D| = \lambda B$, then $E(X) = [1 - (1 + \lambda)P]B$. Hence $E(X) \leq 0$ if $P \geq 1/1+\lambda$. Thus if we imposed a penalty of 99 times the bribe, then it will not be worth being corrupt even if probability of detection is as low as 1 in 100.

greed. Ultimately then the best ideology for a nation is one that blends the pursuit of materials ends with spiritual advancements. *This is the Hindu view of Integral Humanism.*

Democracy is a system of governance of the society. Today about 115 countries have some form of democratic governance. Twenty five years ago, there were only 20 countries. This shows that democracy has become the trend, the accepted system of government globally, and it is spreading world-wide. The view of Lee Kuan Yew of Singapore at one end and Communists at the other, that economic development must be first achieved before democracy is possible, has now been decisively rejected.

Moreover, the comparative economic results in East and West Germany, North and South Korea, China before reform and China now, have conclusively proved that democracy is a better system of governance than dictatorship, and market system is superior to state controlled system.

Devolved democracies also better manage contradictions and conflicts arising out of a heterogeneous society (e.g., India vs. USSR vs. Yugoslavia or Sri Lanka) and provide effective feedback through independent press to enable corrective action by Government (e.g., China's famine). It empowers people to question authority and make them accountable in an election.

But democracy is not a spectator sport for the people. There has to be people's involvement in decision-making and in choosing the right decision-makers. The most dangerous development of the last 61 years in India is the trend amongst the educated people, to despise politics.

For a healthy democracy, educated and well-placed persons, without necessarily formally joining politics, must encourage and help good and learned persons to enter the political arena. Without alert citizens there cannot be transparency and accountability, which are the bed-rock of good governance. Today in India we are hurt by the opaqueness of the decision making process, and we lack a proper system of accountability in all spheres of decision-making. This legitimizes inefficient allocation of scarce resources and encourages corruption. In a comparative economic system framework, India performs poorly in indices of business and corruption.

With the disintegration of the USSR into 16 countries in 1991, comparative economic development theory has changed its focus from a study of alternative systems to alternative governance models of democracy, market system and globalization, i.e., change of focus from dictatorship vs. democracy, and state ownership vs. competitive market, to harmonizing freedom and choice with regulation, how much public sector and how much private, and how the emancipating and enabling power of democracy is to be balanced with the development of a profit-driven and competitive efficient markets i.e. what regulatory democratic institutions must do to promote efficient allocation of resources with good transparent and accountable governance. These harmonizations cannot be achieved unless spiritual values are integrated with the material urges that drive organizations in a new ethos of governance.

With globalization, governance today needs the most sophisticated minds to manage material advancement and prevent it being derailed by greed. Hence spiritual values must legitimize the aspiration of qualified persons to enter politics. This too was our tradition, set out in the Ramayana and the Mahabharata, and followed in the Freedom Movement. But we have lost that tradition today. Persons with no education or those with low educational qualifications are at the helm of affairs today. The few who are educated lack the necessary moral courage to effect accountability and fight corruption.

Just as democracy is favoured by the overwhelming consensus opinion for governance, development is now globally regarded as best done through the market system. Although democracy and market economy conceptually match each other as favouring the freedom of the individuals, it is a volatile mixture, and holds some contradictions. Hence managing these contradictions is a part of good governance and organizational leadership.

For example, democracy empowers the more numerous who are however without much resources i.e., "the poor," while market empowers the well-to-do—"the rich" who are in the minority. Thus, pro-market forces, if selfish, could seek to undermine democracy through crony capitalism or by undermining elections through money power, while the unenlightened and "poor" majority could place curbs on the market through it's voting power.

Democratic development thus needs strong institutions for effective governance. But these institutions should not be so empowered as to be used to threaten democracy in order to be able to contain disorder, and to deal with market failure.

Institutions must thus work out trade-offs such as through just affirmative action, social security and safety nets to create a stake in the market for the poor majority, thus leveling the playing field, and creating hope. This will legitimize reasonable profit-making, thus leading to the harmonization of the market and democracy and resolving the contradictions.

Market-dominant minorities—with their disproportionate capital, skills, business networks, and control over the modern economy—drive globalization. Any backlash against market-dominant minorities, whether the Chinese in Indonesia, Ibo in Nigeria, or political resentment against America at the global level, thus also becomes a backlash against markets, and hence fueling the appeal of the Left politics in these countries.

Thus good governance provides the security for the future stability of the new global system of democracy and market system. This depends on how the market dominant rich minority co-opts the relatively poor majority who dominate the democratic process: because harmonization of contradiction is led by example and not by impersonal institutions. Today we need both democracy and market but by harmonization we must make both work. Hence the art of governance is crucial for our future by resolving the contradiction between democracy and market.

This contradiction if not resolved can electorally doom the best of leaders e.g., P. V. Narasimha Rao. The fact is that today the economic growth in India is indeed lop-sided and requires fresh dynamic vision for reform. For example, how can we explain the fact that while IIM students earn huge salaries, farmers are committing suicides in thousands in the same country?

Governance norms, if properly enforced, can enable India to grow at 12 per cent per year by efficiently using a 36 percent rate of investment by reducing the current incremental capital output ratio from 4.0 to 3.0. A twelve percent growth rate will mean a doubling of GDP every six years and that of per capita income every seven years. This can take us into the league of the top three nations of the world—of the US, China and India—and to overtake China in the next two decades. *That should be the goal of governance for us today.*

India is not yet an economically developed nation. While it has demonstrated prowess in IT software, biotech and pharmaceuticals, accelerated it's growth rate to 9 percent per year to become the third largest nation in terms of GDP at PPP rates, it still has a backward agricultural sector hosting 62 percent of the people of India and in which sector, farmers are committing suicides unable to repay their loans, a national unemployment rate is of over 15 percent of the adult labour force, a prevalence of child labour arising out of nearly fifty percent of the children not making it to school beyond the fifth standard, a deeply malfunctioning primary and secondary educational system, 300 million illiterates and 250 million people in dire poverty; India's infrastructure is pathetic, with frequent electric power break-downs even in metropolitan cities, a dangerously unhealthy water supply in urban areas, galloping HIV infections, and gaping holes on the National Highways.

To become a developed country by 2020, India's GDP will have to grow at 12 percent per year for at least a decade. Technically this is within India's reach, since it would require the rate of investment to rise from the present 28 percent of GDP to 36 percent while productivity growth will have to ensure that the incremental output—capital ratio declines from the present 4.0 to 3.0. These are modest goals that can be attained by increased FDI and by use of IT software in domestic industry. But for that to happen there is required a more vigorous market centric economic reforms to dismantle the vestiges of the Soviet model in Indian planning, especially at the provincial level. The Indian financial system also suffers from a hang-over of cronyism and corruption that have brought the government budgets to the verge of bankruptcy. This too needs fixing. India's infrastructure requires about $ 150 billion dollars to make it world class and the education system needs 6 percent of GDP instead of 2.8 percent today. But an open competitive market system can find these resources provided the quality of governance and accountability is improved. Obviously a second generation of reforms are necessary for all this.

Business ethics if practiced faithfully could be contrary to organizational growth that is fueled by profit maximization—contradictions that are required to be resolved if India is to become a developed country. But there are political compulsions that have to be overcome. Political compulsions that exist are due to electoral politics since the poor in India constitute about 40 percent of the electorate. They are also more conscientious voters and turn out in much higher percentages to vote in elections than do the better—off sections. To succeed in elections, a reformer political leader will have to practice ethical norms but design reforms in such a way that these poor can perceive gains to them as quickly as the vested interests (who are entrenched in the power structure) see their losses. This is not a easy task since upon implementing deregulations, gains from ethical behavior and spiritual values come with a time lag, while loss of 'rents' from controls and quotas that have been vested, are immediate. This is the crux of the challenge of governance. The recent public congregation for prayers for Dr. Ramalinga Raju of Satyam is a case in point: because of his charity, the local community could not care about the national loss from his fraud. Even Dawood Ibrahim, the notorious terrorist, is missed by many in Mumbai.

But reforms are urgently required to be carried out for accelerating India's growth rate to 12 percent per year. India has many advantages today for achieving a booming economy: a demographic dividend, an agriculture that has internationally the lowest yield in land and livestock-based products, and also at the lowest cost of production, a full 12 months a year of farm—friendly weather, a highly competitive skilled labour force and low wage rates at the national level, the advantages of which has already been proved to the world by the outsourcing phenomenon. We have a young population (average is 28 years compared to US of 38 years, and Japan of 49 years) that can be the base for it by ushering innovation in our production process.

Since the world view of economic development has now completely changed, economic development is no more thought of as capital-driven, but as knowledge-driven. For application of knowledge, we need innovations—which means more original research which needs more fresh young minds out—the cream of the youth—to be imbibed with learning and at the frontier of research. This requires adequate empowerment of mental faculty endowed with multi-dimensional intelligence. It is not adequate to foster *cognitive* intelligence only. There are other dimensions of intelligences recognized now viz., *emotional social, moral* and *spiritual.* Our vast youth population is our demographic potential dividend if equipped with multi-dimensional intelligence.

Since Independence in 1947, for decades, we had been told that India's demography was instead her main liability, that India's population was growing too fast, and what India needed most was to control its population, even if by coercive methods.

I had challenged this view as long ago as 1972 that population growth was India's problem [Noted demographer, Dr. Ashish Bose of the University of Delhi had published in 1972 my research as a chapter in his book titled: *India's Population*, in which I had argued that the youth of India would be an asset to the country's development and not a liability]. I argued then that modern science (through the scientific innovations of freshly educated youngsters), can overcome the limitations of land, natural resources and production. I had then also called coercive family planning as "an obsession of developed nations." But the negative view of population prevailed till the "nasbandi" [vasectomy] fiasco of the Emergency in 1975-77 forced Indian politicians to become less vocal about the need for coercive family planning. But the prejudice about population growth in India has continued into the beginning of the 21st century.

Globally, India today leads in the supply of youth, i.e., persons in the age group of 15 to 35 years, and this lead will last for another forty years. We should not therefore squander this "natural resource." We must, by proper policy for the young, realize and harvest this demographic portential. China is the second largest world leader in young population today. But the youth population in that country will start shrinking from 2015, i.e., less than a decade from now because of lagged effect of the one-child policy. Japanese and European total populations are already fast aging, and will start declining in absolute numbers from this year (2009). The US will however hold a steady trend thanks to a liberal policy of immigration, especially from Mexico and Phillipines. But even then the US will have a demographic shortage in skilled personnel. All developed countries will experience a demographic deficit. India will not—if we empower our youth with multiple intelligences. Our past liability, by a fortuitous turn of fate, has now become our potential asset.

Thus, India has now become, by unintended consequences, gifted with a young population. If we educate this youth to develop cognitive intelligence, to become original thinkers, imbibe emotional intelligence to have team spirit and rational risk—taking attitude, inculcate moral intelligence to blend personal ambition with national goals, and cultivate social intelligence to defend civic rights of the weak, gender equality, the courage to fight injustice, and the spiritual intelligence to tap into the cosmic energy that surrounds the earth, then we can develop a superior species of human being, an Indian youth who can be relied on to contribute to make India a global power within two decades.

The nation must therefore structure a national education policy for the youth of India so that in every young Indian, the five dimensional concept of intelligence, viz., cognitive, emotional, moral, social and spiritual, manifests in his or her character. Only then, our demographic dividend will not be wasted. These five dimensions of intelligence constitute the ability of a person to live a productive life and for national good. Hence, a policy for India's youth has to be structured within the implied parameters of these five dimensions.

What are the parameters of such a national policy? These are [1] ability empowerment—that is the development of the five types of intelligence stated above; [2] a collective mindset about the legacy and future of the nation which means knowing the correct de-falsified history of India [3] commitment to a social contract of rights and obligations such as a fundamental right to quality primary and secondary education, right to work, an obligation to compete for positions on merit, practice gender equality and placing national interest above selfish interests.

A National Education Policy is therefore a framework for the comprehensive growth of the nation's young population between 15 and 35 years of age, and for enabling this youth to be positioned in life for personal advancement as well as for contributing to national greatness.

Thus, we lack today a properly structured policy for the development of India's youth. Hence many are going astray to drugs, promiscuity, and crime. Others are going away abroad. There is thus an urgent need for designing such a policy because of the potential that we have to reap the demographic dividend from our large national pool of youth.

I would define an appropriate National Policy as "an architecture" that enables the youth to bloom to the maximum feasible human capacity by the time of attaining full adult maturity. In other words, the architecture consists of *objectives* of youth development, priorities in the attainment of the objectives, a *strategy* based on a coherent agenda to achieve those objectives in the order of priority determined, and mobilization of financial and other resources to implement that strategy. The overall goal of a National Youth Policy has to be to make the nation a secure civilization. All dimensions of development have therefore to be synergized to that goal.

What then are the objectives that the youth should work toward? These objectives cannot be purely materialistic because we know from our past history that though India was the world's most economically developed country, our nation was subject to brutal assault and loot by a handful of foreigners, and for a thousand years we could not rule from Delhi. Materialistic progress alone does not guarantee national security of a nation. What is essential is the character and integrity of its citizens. Hence, besides the objective of acquiring knowledge and getting employment that require cognitive intelligence, the youth must be motivated in other dimensions of intelligence that of emotional, moral and social. These concepts have been developed in the eighteen chapters of the Bhagavad Gita that has been interpreted in modern context by Sri Chandrashekharendra Sarasvati of Kanchi Mutt, Swami Chinmayananda, and Swami Dayananda Sarasvati of Arsha Vidyalaya. In the United States, as the Business Week magazine has recently reported, these concepts have become highly popular in the corporate world, and have been incorporated in the best-selling books written by Daniel Goleman, Deepak Chopra, and Anthony Robbins among others.

Thus, cognitive intelligence is necessary for technical competence and intellectual articulation; emotional intelligence for the ability to perceive, apprise, and express emotion adaptively to create empathy in others, and to regulate emotions in ways that assist thought; moral intelligence is the mental capacity to determine how universal human principles should be applied to our personal values, goals and actions; and social intelligence is knowing how to use our neurological Wi-Fi to motivate others (since our thoughts, emotions and body language impact on the responses of others who interact with us, just as laughter, anger, rebuke, praise, optimism, pessimism, honesty, crookedness, etc., each affects the behaviour of others bilaterally and multilaterally).

In brief, out National Policy for integrating spiritual values and organization leadership can be achieved by measures by which we can create a modern mindset in the youth of India, not only to motivate the youth to acquire technical competence, but to develop emotional, moral, social and spiritual values that will make that person a self-reliant individual of high character, patriotic, and possessing a social conscience. Business ethics and organizational leadership has be founded on that pool of talent.

Such an army of evolved youth will be the asset of the nation; and then collectively the demographic dividend for the nation can be reaped by us for the glory of the nation, Bharat Mata. Hence, a well structured national policy for development of multiple intelligence is vital for making India a global power two decades hence. This, then, would be a basis for our national renewal and renaissance.

Our goal has to be thus the efficient use of resources, human and physical, hardware and software by an able and humane spiritually guided and ethically organizational leadership in a framework of competitive market economies.

But this goal cannot be achieved unless there is accountability in governance: such accountability requires transparent and ethical reporting of the finances of an organization. For this, the ICAI's "Concept Paper on Convergence with IFRS in India" is worth reading. India thus needs to adopt increasingly the International Standards of Financial Reporting and Disclosure Standards for attracting FDI. But that is not the practice today. For example, though SEBI has made compliance for listed companies the Corporate Governance Guidelines mandatory and effective from January 1, 2006, about one-fourth , i.e., 1,213 listed companies have not complied for the period ending March 31, 2008. Yet there has been no action by SEBI, which can under Clause 49 of the Listing Agreement de-list these companies. There is instead a collusion of greedy promoters and chartered accountants. The latest Satyam scandal is only a storm signal of the general and widespread collapse of the values of a corporate system. These failures of governance arises from greed. Greed flourishes where there is no spirituality.

Similarly, as I have pointed out earlier, the Participatory Notes (PN) which account for 55% of the foreign funds into the Stock Market in India have no requirement to comply with even the SEBI disclosure rules, and are obviously meant for laundering the black money of politicians, industrialists and even including those of terrorists. Even after the Tarapore Committee ridiculed the PNs, the SEBI had to keep silent because the Finance Minister favoured P-Notes to launder his ill-gotten money and that of his masters. The lack of ethics and patriotism thus appears maximum inside the government today.

One of the most scandalous frauds on the financial system of India is the derivative called P-Notes. This is to be clubbed with the 'round tripping' of illegal funds—i.e., unaccounted funds of Indians sent to Mauritius by the hawala route and then the illegal funds being brought back to India, taking advantage of the concessions under the Double Taxation Avoidance Treaty, e.g., exemption of Capital Gains tax, both in India and in Mauritius.

In 2002, India and Mauritius extended the controversial Indo-Mauritius Double Taxation Avoidance Treaty (DTAT) first signed in 1983. Under this treaty no resident of Mauritius would be taxed in India on capital gains arising out of the sale of securities in India. In other words, capital gains arising out of sale of shares of securities for an Indian would normally be subject to Capital Gains Tax but, if investments are routed through Mauritius, they would be exempt from the said tax in India. After the DTAT was signed, the Government of Mauritius too abolished capital gains tax in their country. So, in effect, there are no taxes on Mauritius-based FIIs investing in India. After the UPA came to power, Mauritius has emerged as the largest foreign investor in India. *The tax losses to India as a result of the DTAT are estimated at a fabulous Rs.4000 crores to date.*

These two devices: P-Notes and DTAT have enabled financial

buccaneers to rig the Indian stock market giving windfall gains of billions of dollars to racketeers, and spelling ruin for the middle class.

An example of this is when some foreign investors sold stocks aggregating to Rs.18000+crores on just 2 days viz., January 23 and 24, 2008. I quote a media report of that time: "In the third week of 2008, the Sensex experienced huge falls along with other markets around the world. On 21 January, 2008, the Sensex saw its highest loss of 1,408 points at the end of the session.... The next day, the Sensex index went into a free fall. It hit the lower circuit breaker a minute after the markets opened at 10 AM. Trading was therefore suspended an hour. On re-opening at 10.55 AM, the market saw its biggest ever fall when it hit a low of 15,332, down 2,273 points. However on "reassurance" from the Finance Minister of India, the market back to close at 16,730 with a loss of 875 points." Today, the Sensex is below 10,000. Who are the beneficiaries?

In his address to the 43rd Munich Conference on Security Policy on February 11, 2007, M. K. Narayanan, the National Security Advisor to the Government of India, listed out the various ways by which terrorists in India were funded. He admitted: "Instances of terrorist outfits manipulating the stock markets to raise funds for their operations have been reported. Stock exchanges in Mumbai and Chennai have, on occasion, reported that fictitious or notional companies were engaging in stock market operations. Some of these companies were later traced to terrorist outfits." This is a truly shocking admission.

Thus, as the Government of India is well aware, terrorists are parking funds in Indian ventures. Yet the Finance Ministry has done nothing about the system of P-notes, which gives terrorists the additional benefit of anonymity while making hefty investments in the Indian market, which could later be used to fund terrorist activities against the Indian people in India! According to conservative estimates, there are over Rs. 3,50,000 Crore Rupees worth of P-notes issued abroad by FIIs and brokers being actively traded in the Indian market! At present P-Notes fuels about 53% of all foreign investments in the stock markets of India.

The notional value of investment in Participatory Notes [PNs] which aggregated to Rs. 31,875 crores in over 10 years up to March 2004, grew to Rs. 3,53,484 crores by August 2007—that is by over 11 times in just 40 months! It was this financial device which transmitted the US banks collapse and sub-prime crisis to India. In September 2008—January 2009 $61 billion in re-purchased PNs fled the country causing the dollar to appreciate from Rs. 38 to Rs. 52 (while the dollar was depreciating everywhere else in the world.)

The investment through PN constituted 20% of all FII investment in 2004. This increased to over 51.6% in August 2007. Thus by 2007, more than half the FII investments in India were through the anonymous PN formula.

The sub-accounts created by the FII for these nameless entities not registered with SEBI, is fraught with dangerous consequences and security risk. The sources of these funds are unknown since the investors are nameless; the billions of dollars invested through PNs are address-less, and the SEBI has been barred from probing by the Ministry of Finance. Why?

Thus, the "know Your Customer" prudential norms, which the law makes it mandatory for opening of even simple banks accounts by Indians in India, are not followed in permitting billions of dollars of investment into the stocks markets in India!

The PN mechanism—through which unnamed investors are allowed to participate in our markets, invest and disinvest stocks for billions of dollars and make and repatriate profits—is thus a mystery wrapped in a puzzle, packed in an enigma, crammed inside a conundrum and delivered through a riddle.

The clamour for this form of investment is patently intriguing, if not outright suspicious. It was felt by many experts that PN's are the Weapons of Mass Destruction—WMD—of our stock markets, and it has proved itself by the artificial and induced peaks and troughs of the Sensex.

To date, the nation is not aware of any details whatsoever of the investors who seek to invest through P-Notes, which under the present regulations, permits such investors to remain anonymous. This is unprecedented in any democratic nation. Also the people have no data on Indian plutocrats who are re-routing their unaccounted money through Mauritius, cleverly avoiding Capital Gains Tax both in that country and ours by taking advantage of the Indo-Mauritius Double Taxation Avoidance Treaty.

The Union Finance Ministry had in a press note claimed: "FIIs are regulated entities; SEBI being the regulator ... FIIs are required to report at the end of every month, in the prescribed format, all the information relating to P-notes issued by them including the names of subscribers to the said P-notes." [rebuttal dated 5.6.2008 of Ms. J. Jayalalithaa's press statement].

From this, one has to assume that SEBI has the names and details of all the foreign investors who have invested in India through these P-Notes. If this is the stated position, the Union Finance Ministry ought to furnish answers to the question about the identity of P-Notes owners.

But the Union Finance Ministry has refused to publish the list of P-note holders, along with their details and the amount of investment, on its website, or on the website of SEBI, or anywhere else.

P-notes are subscribed to by a company but the Union Finance Ministry does not track the names of the owners/promoters/ beneficiaries of that company. Hence the company in question could well be promoted or funded by an Osama bin-Laden, a Dawood Ibrahim or a Velupillai Pirabhakaran? If so, how to ensure that narco-terrorist money does not find its way into the

Annexure from SEBI's website

Daily Trends in FII Investments for January, 2008

	Debt/Equity	Gross Purchase (Rs Crores)	Gross Sales (Rs Crores)	Net Investment (Rs Crores)	Net Investment US ($) million at month exchange rate
01-JAN-2008	Equity	3041.10	2243.30	797.90	197.80
	Debt	6.50	18.00	(11.50)	(2.90)
02-JA	Equity	1437.60	1295.30	142.30	35.30
	Debt	0.00	3.00	(3.00)	(0.70
OJ-JAN- 2008	Equity	4083.80	4328.30	(244.50)	(60.60)
	Debt	93.30	182.90	(89.60)	(22.20)
04-JAN-2008	Equity	6007.10	5281.90	725.10	179.80
	Debt	390.90	3.00	387.90	96.20
07-JAN-2008	Equity	4549.40	4040.60	508.80	126.10
	Debt	730.80	209.80	521.00	129.20
08-JAN-2008	Equity	4891.40	4972.30	(80.90)	(20.10)
	Debt	104.60	242.60	(138.00)	(34.20)
09-JAN- 2008	Equity	5529.90	4476.50	1053.40	261.10
	Debt	744.00	86.80	657.20	162.90
1 Q-JAN-2008	Equity	4859.70	4585.10	274.60	68.10
	Debt	677.70	605.70	72.00	17.90
Il-JAN-2008	Equity	4334.20	4965.00	(630.80)	(156.40)
	Debt	580.60	295.20	285.40	70.70
14-JAN-2008	Equity	3906.30	3792.60	113.70	28.20
	Debt	318.70	85.00	233.70	57.90
15-JAN-2008	Equity	4521.50	4347.20	174.40	43.20
	Debt	241.90	119.40	122.40	30.40
16-JAN-2008	Equity	5209.90	4984.10	225.80	56.00
	Debt	249.10	45.10	204.00	50.60
17 -JAN-2008	Equity	4662.30	6941.90	(2279.60)	(565.10)
	Debt	81.80	182.50	(100.80)	(25.00)
18-JAN-2008	Equity	4303.30	6489.30	(2186.00)	(541.90)
	Debt	78.50	422.40	(343.80)	(85.20)
21-JAN-2008	Equity	4972.30	6328.40	(1356.10)	(336.20)
	Debt	78.40	103.30	(24.90)	(6.20)
22-JAN-2008	Equity	4896.90	7322.50	(2425.70)	(601.30)
	Debt	142.40	236.40	(93.90)	(23.30)
23-JAN-2008	Equity	7749.20	10005.50	(2256.20)	(559.30)
	Debt	116.30	487.40	(371.10)	(92.00)
24-JAN-2008	Equity	6082.50	8582.30	(2499.90)	(619.70)
	Debt	662.00	28.00	634.10	157.20
25-JAN-2008	Equity	5347.20	6698.40	(1351.20)	(335.00)
	Debt	70.80	49.60	21.30	5.30
28-JAN-2008	Equity	4854.60	4185.60	669.10	165.90
	Debt	0.00	0.00	0.00	0.00
29-JAN-2008	Equity	2600.30	4113.60	(1513.40)	(375.20)
	Debt	288.10	296.60	(8.60)	(2.10)
30-JAN-2008	Equity	2924.50	3209.60	(285.10)	(70.70)
	Debt	0.00	0.00	0.00	0.00
31-JAN-2008	Equity	2913.20	3524.60	(611.40)	(151.60)
	Debt	0.00	0.00	0.00	0.00
Total for January	Equity	103678.20	116713.90	(13035.70)	(3231.60)
	Debt	5656.40	3702.70	1953.80	484.50
Total for 2008	Equity	103678.30	116713.90	(13035.60)	(3231.50)
	Debt	5656.40	3702.60	1953.80	484.40
Grand Total till January 31, 2008	Equity	2247994.80	1977562.20	270432.80	63097.60
	Debt	80039.30	62236.10	17803.50	4109.70

No of Registered FII's :1279 as on 31.01.2008.

No of Registered Sub-accounts: 3795 as on 31.01.2008

	Gross Purchases (Rs Crores)	Gross Sales (Rs Crores)	Net Investment (Rs Crores)	Net Investment US($) million at month exchange rate
Prior period adjustments Equity	3518.41	87.66	3430.75	773.91

The above adjustments are due to migration of data of new sub accounts to portal based new system of reporting.

18th Apr. 2008 is a non-trading day. The figures corresponding to 18th Apr. 2008 are also to be included for the reporting date of 17th Apr. 2008.

The above report is compiled on the basis of reports submitted to SEBI by custodians on January 31, 2008 and constitutes trades conducted by FIIs on and upto the previous trading day(s).

Discrepancies in total figures, if any, are due to rounding off.

Indian Stock Market, as the National Security Advisor M. K. Narayan had feared?

M. Damodaran, who had headed SEBI, had told the *Business Standard* (in September, 2007), that he was not "entirely confortable" that one-fourth of the market was being held by anonymous P-note investors." He told me so personally too.

The idea to introduce P-Notes and the Mauritius round-tripping facility for hawala route for illegal funds of politicians, criminals and terrorists was the brain child of the NDA Government Finance Minister Yashwant Sinha of Gold Auction fame of 1991. Some of us may remember that, on the assumption of office by Dr. Manmohan Singh the UPA Government on May 18, 2004, it was greeted with a steep fall in the Indian Stock Market (Sensex fell by 567.74 points). It was *later* found that UBS Securities Asia Ltd, which is a SEBI registered FII dealing through its SEBI registered proprietary sub-account Swiss Finance Corporation (Mauritius) Ltd, *had sold stocks* in the Cash Market segment to the extent of Rs.188.35 crores. SEBI decided to investigate. During the investigation, SEBI called for further information from UBS relating to its major P-note clients in terms of their addresses, the names of their directors, fund managers, major shareholders, top five investors etc., UBS did not furnish the information citing reasons such as client confidentially. This is a substantiated allegation that I am making, since I am basing it on what is contained in SEBI Order No. WTM/GA/1/STD/5/05.

But the Union Finance Ministry has taken no action since May 2004 [when the UPA Government assumed office] to arm SEBI with appropriate legal teeth to face such situations in future. On the contrary, it took P-Notes out of the purview of SEBI much to the dismay of the Tarapore Committee on Financial Reforms.

The Report of the Expert Group on Encouraging FII Flows and Checking the Vulnerability of Capital Markets to Speculative Flows of the Reserve Bank of India, sent to Dr. Ashok Lahiri, Chief Economic Adviser, Department of Economic Affairs, Ministry of Finance, Government of India, states: "The Reserve Bank's stance has been that the issue of Participatory Notes *should not be permitted.* In this context we would like to point out that the main concerns regarding issue of PNs are that the nature of the beneficial ownership or the identity of the investor will not be known, unlike in the case of FIIs registered with a financial regulator. Trading of these PNs will lead to multi-layering which will make it difficult to identify the ultimate holder of PNs. Both conceptually and in practice, restrictions on suspicious flows enhance the reputation of markets and lead to healthy flows."

This capacity for mischief by using P-Notes was revealed when foreign investors had sold stocks on the 23rd and 24th January 2008, aggregating to Rs. 18,600 crores. Who are these people who sold stocks in such massive quantities, which led to an unprecedented fall of the Indian stock market on these two days, leading to unprecedented huge losses to the ordinary Indian investors, even leading to suicides by several investors who lost all? And why? Soon thereafter, new mysterious buyers with P-Note holders arrived and bought these stocks at crashed prices. And because of the Mauritius routing for the purchase, no capital gains could be levied.

SEBI in fact had, in September 2006, slapped a fine of Rs.1 crore on Goldman Sachs Investment (Mauritius) for the latter's failure to report the issuance of P-notes to the Mauritius-based Magnus Capital Corporation Ltd. This was considered a violation of the declaration to furnish regular statements to SEBI on the P-notes issued by them. However, on May 5, 2008, the Securities Appellate Tribunal (SAT), set aside SEBI's order against Goldman Sachs Mauritius. It opined that SEBI was not at all justified in asking FIIs and their sub-accounts to file undertakings of the kind prescribed in the revised reporting format contained in the circular of August 8, 2003. It also overturned SEBI's fine of $1 crore, and instead asked the official market regulator SEBI to pay Rs.1 lakh to Goldman Sachs for harassing them!!

The case is not only a slap on the face of SEBI, but also a clear indication that the Union Finance Minister's claim that investments from abroad are being adequately monitored by SEBI is false and deliberately misleading.

Set out hereinbelow, is the order passed in this matter by SAT:

BEFORE THE SECURITIES APPELLATE TRIBUNAL,
MUMBAI

Appeal No. 153 of 2006
Date of decision: 15.5.2008

Goldman Sachs Investments (Mauritius) Limited .... Appellant

Versus

The Adjudicating Officer,
Securities and Exchange Board of India ...... Respondent

Mr. Darius Khambatta Senior Counsel with Ms. Ipshita Dutta Advocate for Appellant.

Mr. J.J. Bhatt Senior Advocate with Dr. Poornima Advani Advocate and Ms. Sejal Shah Advocate for Respondent.

Coram: Justice N.K. Sodhi, Presiding Officer
Arun Bhargava, Member
Utpal Bhattacharya, Member

Per: Justice N.K. Sodhi, Presiding Officer

The primary question that arises for our consideration in this Appeal is whether the Securities and Exchange Board of India (hereinafter called the Board) could ask the Foreign Institutional Investors (FIIs) to furnish an undertaking that they had not dealt in respect of off-shore derivative instruments with Indian residents, non-resident Indians (NRIs) persons of Indian origin (PIOs) or overseas corporate bodies (OCBs) in the absence of a bar on such deals.

2. With a view to regulate the activities of FIIs and their sub-accounts, the Board framed the Securities and Exchange Board of India (Foreign Institutional Investors) Regulations, 1995 (for short the Regulations). These provide that no person shall buy, sell or otherwise deal in securities as an FII unless he holds a certificate granted by the Board under the Regulations. An FII is also required to seek from the Board registration of each sub-account on whose behalf he proposes to make investments in India. Regulation 20 enjoins that every FII shall, as and when required by the Board or the Reserve Bank of India, submit to the Board or the Reserve Bank of India, as the case may be, any information, record or documents in relation to its activities as an FII. The Board found that some FIIs were issuing derivatives/financial instruments against underlying Indian securities under different names such as participatory notes, equity linked notes etc. In order to monitor the investments by FIIs through these derivatives/financial instruments, the Board decided that FIIs should report the issuance/renewal/cancellation/redemption of these instruments to it and accordingly, issued a circular dated October 31, 2001 prescribing the format in which the report was to be submitted. The Board further advised that the report shall be submitted by only those FIIs which issue such instruments and that the reports were to be submitted only on issuance/renewal/cancellation/redemption of the aforesaid instruments and only for the month(s) during which the FIIs had issued/renewed/cancelled/redeemed those instruments. These reports were required to be submitted on a monthly basis within a week of the end of the month duly signed and approved by the compliance officer. By a Subsequent circular dated August 8, 2003 the Board decided to revise the format for reporting the issuance/renewal/cancellation/redemption of derivatives/financial instruments. The report was to be submitted in two forms

which were enclosed with this circular as Annexures A and B. For the first time the reporting format included an undertaking. Annexure A is a one time report to be submitted once only in which the FII is required to indicate the outstanding off-shore derivatives as on August 15, 2003. After finishing the requisite information in the one time report, the FII or the sub-account, as the case may be, is required to furnish the following undertaking :

"We undertake that we/associates/clients have not issued/subscribed/purchased any of the offshore derivative instruments directly or indirectly to/from Indian residents/ NRls/PIOs/OCBs."

Information as required by Annexure B was to be submitted for every fortnight from the first day of the month to the 15th day of the same month and from 16th day of the month till the last day of the month. The reporting in Annexure B commenced with effect from the fortnight ending August 31, 2003. The information for each fortnight is required to be submitted within three working days from the closure of the fortnight. The fortnightly report is also required to contain an undertaking by the FII or the sub-account, as the case may be, in the following words:

"We undertake that we/associates/clients have not issued/ subscribed/purchased any of the off-shore derivative instruments directly or indirectly to/from Indian residents/NRIs/PIOs/OCBs during the Statement Period."

This circular revising the format tor reporting was also issued under Regulation 20 of the Regulations.

3. Goldman Sachs Investments (Mauritius) Limited—the appellant herein is a registered sub-account with the Board and Goldman Sachs & Co. is the registered FII. On November 25, 2002, the appellant as a sub-account issued off-shore derivative instruments (ODIs), among others, to its affiliate namely, Goldman Sachs International Ltd. England with the shares of Himachal Futuristic Communications Ltd. as the underlying security. The affiliate in turn issued ODIs on the same underlying security on a back to back basis to Magnus Capital Corporation Limited (for short Magnus) which is an OCB. At the time when these ODIs had been issued, the revised format for reporting had not been prescribed. However, on the issuance of the circular dated August 8, 2003, the appellant was obliged to submit the one time report indicating the total outstanding off-shore derivatives as on August 15, 2003 in the prescribed form in Annexure A to the circular. This report was filed with a forwarding letter dated August 20, 2003. The report was incomplete and the difficulties experienced by the appellant in furnishing the complete information were mentioned in the accompanying letter.

However, the complete information was furnished to the Board on August 29, 2003 through e-mail. It is pertinent to note that the one time report which was submitted to the Board in two parts did not contain the undertaking which

Annexure A to the circular had prescribed. In addition to the information in Annexure A, the appellant was required to file fortnightly reports as envisaged in Annexure B to the circular as and when ODIs were/are issued/renewed/cancelled/redeemed. The appellant was filing the fortnightly reports as and when required with the following undertaking:

"Goldman Sachs Investment (Mauritius) International Ltd., undertake on behalf of itself and its affiliates (Goldman Sachs) that as far as it is aware, Goldman Sachs has not entered into any offshore derivatives on Indian Underlyers directly with Indian Residents, NRIs or OCB's (each as defined under relevant Indian laws and regulations) during the statement period. As agreed with SEBI, this undertaking does not extends to persons of Indian Origin, whether comprising part of the above categories of persons or otherwise."

The undertaking given by the appellant is substantially different from the one prescribed in Annexure B. It is the case of the appellant that the undertaking as prescribed could not be given and that its representatives had been meeting and coresponding with the officers of the Board on the basis of which they worked out an acceptable arrangement by which the aforementioned modified undertaking was being furnished. It is, thus, clear that in the one time report which was submitted in two parts, the appellant did not file any undertaking whereas in its fortnightly reports an undertaking in a modified form was being furnished

4. In the light of the reports filed by the appellant, the Board was of the opinion that the former had violated the circular dated August 8, 2003 and Regulation 13(1) of the Regulations and, therefore, initiated adjudication proceedings under Chapter VIA of the securities and Exchange Board of India Act, 1992 (hereinafter called the Act). The adjudicating officer served a notice dated June 6, 2006 calling upon the appellant to show cause why penalty be not imposed in terms of section 15HB of the Act. The appellant filed a detailed reply controverting the allegations made in the notice. It was pointed out that it had neither violated the reporting circular nor Regulation 13(1). The adjudicating officer framed the following three issues which, according to him, arose from the show cause notice and the reply:

"6.1 Whether the Undertaking given by GSIML is false/OR, GSIML violated the declaration regarding issuance of ODIs;

6.2 Whether GSIML violated the provisions of Regulation 20 of FII Regulations; and

6.3 Whether Regulation 13(1) of FII Regulation is attracted in the instant matter."

Issues no.1 & 2 were decided against the appellant in the following words:

"... From the bare perusal of the aforesaid undertaking given by the notice is made out that the undertaking was not at all in the format prescribed by the SEBI in its circular dated August 8, 2003. At many places in the reply of the notice, I find a mention about notice seeking clarification from SEBI and also their ignorance of law about prohibition on dealing with OCB's, because of which they did not include the undertaking in the first statement but later it was included in a statement filed in continuation of the first statement. I can understand that the notice was consciously aware of the importance of the declaration and that is why firstly it avoided filing declaration. So according to me, this is an occasion when the noticee first violated the SEBI circular by not providing the declaration and later when after all of its so called discussions/clarifications from SEBI (the details of the outcome of which is not furnished by the noticee), the noticee claims to have complied with SEBI circular by filing a declaration entirely different from the prescribed format. In this connection, I would like to strongly object to the move of the noticee to amend/change the prescribed format of the undertaking as per the SEBI circular, to suit to its liking. At the outset, if this is the way a registered entity complies with the SEBI circular, I would say it is no compliance. Secondly, on the issue of MCCL being an OCB it is clearly observed from the communication from the Reserve Bank of India (RBI) dated December 26, 2003 addressed to SEBI (Annexure D of the SCN) that Magnus Capital Corporation. Mauritius is an Overseas Corporate Body (OCB). The noticee cannot be allowed to plead an ignorance of this fact. The noticee that is Goldman Sachs, having its presence in the financial/capital sectors world wide, is expected to have compliances of highest level, and which is found lacking in the instant matter. It seems that the noticee has failed to give any significance to the information to be given to the Regulator, on the ODI's issued to OCB's. It is a common knowledge and fact that OCB's had mis-utilised ODI route to park their illegal money and to manipulate Indian securities market without the fear of their identity getting detected. So the issues framed at paras 6.1 and 6.2 above are decided to the effect that the noticee has violated the declaration furnished in the fortnightly statement on issue of ODI's submitted to SEBI (As on August 15, 2603) ...."

Issue no.3 pertaining to the violation of Regulation 13(1) was held to be only incidental to the main charge of furnishing a false declaration and was answered against the appellant as under:

"... I am of the view that the purpose of this proviso, barring OCB's to invest as sub-account or as FII in Indian securities market, can only be met with, if OCB's are also denied making, investments as clients of sub-account or FII otherwise the legislative intent and the object of the provision would get defeated. In the instant matter, the noticee has defeated the purpose of the proviso to Regulation 13(1) (b) by issuing ODI's to OCB's....

By his order dated September 8, 2006, the adjudicating officer imposed a penalty of Rs. one crore on the appellant under section 15 HB of the Act. It is against this order that the present appeal has been filed.

5. let us first deal with the primary question posed in the beginning of our order which is whether the Board was at all justified in asking the FIIs and the sub-accounts to file undertakings of the kind prescribed in the revised reporting format contained in the circular of August 8, 2003. D.J. Khambatta learned senior counsel for the appellant strenuously argued that till such time the circular was issued there was no bar on the FIIs and their sub-accounts to deal in ODIs with Indian residents/NRIs/ PIOs/OCBs and that many of them had been dealing with them in the past and, therefore, the Board could not by this circular in question require such FIIs/sub-accounts to furnish an undertaking that they had not dealt with such persons. We find considerable force in this contention. In view of the economic reforms introduced in the country and with the opening up of the Indian securities market to the foreign participants, it became necessary for the Board to keep itself abreast of their activities and monitor the same. It is with this object in view that Regulation 20 enjoins upon the FIIs to submit to the Board any information, record or documents in relation to their activities as and when required. Regulation 20A was introduced on 28.8.2003 making it further clear that the FIIs shall fully disclose the information concerning the terms of and parties to the ODIs entered into by them or by their sub-accounts or affiliates relating to securities listed or proposed to be listed in any stock exchange in India. It was in pursuance to the powers conferred by Regulation 20 that the circular dated October 31, 2001 was issued requiring FIIs to report the issuance/renewal/cancellation/redemption of the derivatives/financial instruments against underlying Indian securities issued by them. Since there was no bar on the FIIs and their sub-accounts to issue/subscribe/purchase any derivative instrument to/from Indian residents/NRls/PIOs/OCBs, it would be reasonable to presume that many of them must have dealt with such persons in the course of their business activities. When this was the position, the Board suddenly amended the reporting requirements by the FIIs and their sub-accounts on August 8, 2003 by prescribing the revised reporting format to which a detailed reference has already been made requiring them to furnish an undertaking with effect from the date of the circular that they had not dealt in ODIs with Indian residents/NRls/PIOs/OCBs in the past. We wonder how they could be asked to furnish such an undertaking in the absence of any bar to deal with such persons. This requirement of an undertaking appears to us to be opposed to all norms of reason and is totally devoid of logic. In fact, it borders on absurdity and is arbitrary. When the FIIs and their sub-accounts have not been debarred from dealing in ODIs with Indian residents/ NRIs/PIOs/OCBs and many of them would have dealt with the latter, they could not be asked to furnish the undertaking. We could have appreciated the requirement of the undertaking being given by FIIs and their sub-accounts only if they had first been debarred from dealing with the aforesaid persons. In other words, the bar must necessarily precede the undertaking demanded from the FIIs and their sub-accounts. The learned senior counsel for the appellant further contended that even as on today

there is no provision either in the Act or in the Regulations which debars FIIs or their sub-accounts from dealing in ODIs with Indian residents/NRIs/PIOs/OCBs. The learned senior counsel, however, brought to our notice Regulation 15A of the Regulations which was inserted on 3.2.2004 and the same reads as under:

"15A (1) A Foreign Institutional Investor or sub-account may issue, dealing or hold, off-shore derivative instruments such as Participatory Notes, Equity Linked Notes or any other similar instruments against underlying securities, listed or proposed to be listed on any stock exchange in India, only in favour of those entities which are regulated by any relevant regulatory authority in the countries of their incorporation or establishment, subject to compliance of "know your client" requirement.

Provided that if any such instrument has already been issued. prior to the 3rd February, 2004, to a person other than a regulated entity, contract for such transaction shall expire on maturity of the instrument or within a period of five years from the 3rd February, 2004, whichever is earlier.

15HB. Whoever fails to comply with any provision of this Act, the rules or the regulations made or directions issued by the Board thereunder for which no separate penalty has been provided, shall be liable to a penalty which may extend to one crore rupees...."

We have repeatedly gone through the allegations made in para 3 of the show cause notice and those have not made us wiser. We are unable to ascertain as to what is the precise charge which the adjudicating officer was wanting to make out. Para 3 of the notice when carefully read apparently means this: The appellant as a sub-account had issued ODIs to Magnus which is an OCB and "thereby violated the declaration furnished in the fortnightly statement on issue of off-shore derivative instruments submitted to SEBI (as on August 15, 2003—copy enclosed).... Therefore, it is alleged that you have dealt with an OCB and gave an incorrect declaration that...."

As already noticed, the revised reporting format prescribed by the circular dated August 8, 2003 required two reports to be furnished in Annexures A and B. In para 3 of the show cause notice what is alleged is the violation of the fortnightly report as on August 15, 2003. There is no fortnightly report as on 15.8.2003. The report as on 15.8.2003 is the one time report and not the fortnightly report. One cannot, therefore, make out as to which of the two reports the adjudicating officer is referring to and which is the declaration that is said to have been violated. This is why we say the show cause notice is confusing. Be that as it may, a copy of the report the declaration in which was allegdly violated had been enclossd with the show cause notice. That report was the one time report submitted by the appellant in Annexure A. One could then presume that the adjudicating ofticer was alleging the violation of the declaration made in the one time report. The one time report was submitted by the appellant In two parts - on August 20 and 29, 2003. Interestingly, none of those reports contain any declaration/ undertaking at all and this fact is not only admitted but the adjudicating officer himself has recorded a finding to that effect in the impugned order. How could it then be said that the appellant violated the declaration made in the one time report when there is none. We could have appreciated if it had been alleged that the appellant failed to furnish the prescribed declaration/untertaking in the one time report but that is not the charge. Faced with this situation, Shri J.J. Bhatt learned senior counsel for the Board submitted that the show cause notice when properly read levels the charge that the appellant failed to furnish the undertaking in Annexure A. If we accept this contention, we would be modifying the charge at the appellate stage which is impermissible. Moreover, the adjudicating officer has levied the penalty for furnishing a false declaration and not for failure to furnish one. Even if one were to assume that reference in para 3 of the show cause notice is to the fortnightly report and not to the one time report (though there is no warrant for the same because copy of the one time report had been sent along with the notice), the charge of violating the declaration cannot stand. One is left guessing as to which fortnightly report the adjudicating officer is referring to. Since he has mentioned 15.8.2003 as the date in the show cause notice and even if we presume that he is referring to a fortnightly statement of August 2003, it could only be the second fortnightly statement. This statement contained the modified undertaking already referred to in the earlier part of the order to the effect that as far as the appellant was aware, it did not enter into any ODI with any Indian resident, NRI or OCB during the statement period. This declaration is not incorrect because during this fortnight the appellant did not issue, renew, cancel or redeem any ODI.

From whatever angle we may look at, the charge of filing an incorrect declaration cannot stand. Moreover, there are too many assumptions that one has to make before the charge can be spelt out. At this stage it would be appropriate to refer to the observations of the Supreme Court in Canara Bank and others vs Debasis Das and others (2003) 4 SEC 557. This is what the learned judges have laid down:

"The adherence to principles of natural justice as recognized by all civilized States is of supreme importance when a quasi-judicial body embarks on determining disputes between the parties, or any administrative action involving civil consequences is in issue. These principles are well settled. The first and foremost principle is what is commonly known as audi alterarn partem rule. It says that no one should be condemned unheard. Notice is the first limb of this principle. It must be precise and unambiguous. It should apprise the party determinatively of the case he has to meet.

Time given for the purpose should be adequate so as to enable him to make his representation. In the absence of a notice of the kind and such reasonable opportunity the order passed becomes wholly vitiated. Thus, it is but essential that a party should be put on notice of the case before any adverse order is passed against him. This is one of the most important principles of natural justice. It is after all an approved rule of fair play. The concept has gained significance and shades with time." (emphasis supplied) These observations apply with full force to the facts of our case. In view of what we have said above, we have no hesitation in holding that the show cause notice is not only vague and confusing but also self contradictory and the impugned order deserves to be set aside on this ground as well.

9. The adjudicating officer has taken exception to the modified declaration/Undertaking given by the appellant in all its fortnightly statements. It was strenuously urged by the learned senior counsel for the appellant that the modified form of the declaration was/is being furnished after obtaining the consent of the officers of the Board and, therefore, initiating adjudication proceedings was not justified. There is merit in this contention as well. There is no gainsaying the fact that the undertakings given by the appellant in its fortnightly statements are not in conformity with the prescribed format. What happened was that soon after the circular dated August 8, 2003 was issued prescribing the revised reporting format and after the appellant had filed its incomplete one time report, the Board addressed a communication dated 27.8.2003 requiring the appellant to explain why it had omitted to give the undertaking and sought some additional information. In response thereto, the representative of the appellant contacted Santosh Sharma the then Divisional chief of FII department of the Board on August 28, 2003 and explained to him the difficulties which the appellant and other industry participants were facing with the prescribed form of undertaking. It appears that Sharma agreed with the appellant that the undertaking in the prescribed format could not be given and that the appellant could exclude PIOs from its undertaking. As agreed to between them, the appellant filed its fortnightly reports giving the modified undertaking (as quoted in the second part of para 3 of the show cause notice and reproduced in the earlier part of our order) and the same is being filed till date. The representatives of the appellant again met Santosh Sharma on October 9, 2003 and the latter confirmed that he had no issue with the modified undertaking which the appellant had been filing. While the discussions between the representatives of the appellant and the Board were continuing, the latter issued a show cause notice to the former under section 11B of the Act alleging that it had violated the circular dated August 8, 2003 in as much as it did not file the undertaking as per the prescribed format. Proceedings in regard to this show cause notice are still pending. It appears that by this time, Mr. Santosh Sharma was no longer the Divisional chief of FII department and the appellant raised its concerns in early November 2003 in a meeting with two officers of the Board namely Batra and Natrajan who also, according to the appellant, were sympathetic to the problems pointed out by the latter. The appellant filed its reply on November 13, 2003 to the notice received under section 11B of the Act and has relied upon the aforesaid discussions. On November 19, 2003 the representative of the appellant met Chanda the new Divisional chief of FII department of the Board to clarify, among other issues, the

modification of the prescribed undertaking. The appellant then recorded all the discussions it had with Chanda and earlier with Santosh Sharma and sent an e-mail on November 20, 2003 to Chanda in confirmation thereof. A ropy of this detailed e-mail is on the record which has not been disputed. Thereafter, the appellant had some telephonic conversation with Chanda who agreed that tile appellant could file the modified undertaking. This telephonic conversation was also confirmed by Chanda as per his e-mail dated December 2, 2003 sent 10 the appellant. In view of this documentary material on the record which was not disputed by the learned senior counsel appearing for the Board, we have no hesitation in holding that the officers of the Board of the rank of Divisional chief of FII department had permitted the appellant to file the undertaking in the modified format in which it was actually submitted. In this view of the matter, it cannot be said that the appellant violated the prescribed format of the undertaking. If at all it did, it did so with the clear permission of the Board and the latter is not justified in levelling the charge now in issue. The adjudicating officer was not justified in observing that there was no material on the record to substantiate the discussions referred to herein above. Obviously, he has not looked at the record.

10. We may now deal with yet another aspect of the charge that could be discerned from the show cause notice. If we have understood correctly, the charge is that the appellant dealt with Magnus which is an OCB and thereby violated the proviso to Regulation 13(1) of the Regulations which reads as under:

"Procedure and grant of registration of sub-accounts.

13(1). For the purpose of grant of registration the Board shall take into account all matters Which are relevant to the grant of such registration to the sub-account and in particular the following, namely:

(a) ....

(b) ....

Provided that a non-resldent Indian or an overseas corporate body registered with Reserve Bank of India shall not be eligible to invest as sub-account or as foreign institutional investor."

The fact that Magnus is an OCB and that the appellant dealt with it through its affiliate is not in dispute. However, this charge must fail on two counts. Firstly, the proviso reproduced above debars a non-resident Indian or an OCB from investing in India only "as sub-account or as foreign institutional investor." It is nobody's case that Magnus has invested in India either as a sub-account or as FII and, therefore, the bar envisaged in the proviso to Regulation 13(1) is not attracted. The observations made by the adjudicating officer in para 11 of the impugned order the relevant part of which have been reproduced in para 4 of our order can only be described as absurd and betray his inability to understand the plain language of the proviso to Regulation 13(1). In his eagerness to decide this issue against the appellant, he has attempted to rewrite the Regulation. Secondly, it is the case of the appellant that when it issued the

ODIs in November 2002, it did not know that Magnus was an OCB, OCBs wanting to carry on activities in India are registered with the Reserve Bank of India and it is that Bank which maintains their list. The appellant contends, and we are in agreement with its learned senior counsel that the list of OCBs is not in the public domain nor is it on the website of the Reserve Bank of India and, therefore, not easily accessible to anyone or everyone. It is clear from the record that even the Board came to know that Magnus was an OCB only when it received the letter dated December 26, 2003 from the Reserve Bank of India. This letter is a pan of the show cause notice issued to the appellant and we have perused the same. It appears to us that even the Reserve Bank of India before confirming that Magnus was an OCB took up the matter with the designated Bank of OCB i.e. Hongkong and Shanghai Banking Corporation Ltd. When the Board itself was not aware and the Reserve Bank of India was not clear about the status of Magnus till December 2003, we do not think that it was fair and reasonable to charge the appellant for having dealt with Magnus as OCB.

11. When the circular dated August 8, 2003 was issued the appellant and, may be, some others as well, found that it may not be possible for them to comply with its requirements in view of the incongruities referred to hereinabove and sought some clarification from the Board. This is what the appellant said in its letter dated August 20, 2003 which is relevant for our purpose:

"With reference to the undertaking that SEBI has requested at the bottom of the report we would like to understand from SEBI the reason for providing this Undertaking. It is our understanding that there are no restrictions under regulations applicable to FIIs with respect to whom offshore affiliates of FIIs/sub-accounts may enter into any transactions. We would be grateful if SEBI could provide some clarification in this regard."

The adjudicating officer seems to have taken offence to the clarification sought by the appellant and observed in para 9 of the impugned order as under:

"... On the face of it, questioning the requirement of a provision, from the regulator who is exercising its lawful powers under the Takeover Regulations is something inconceivable."

The clarification sought by the appellant was obviously reasonable as it is really not understandable as to why the Board asked the FIIs to file the undertaking in the prescribed format. Instead of furnishing some plausible response to the clarification sought, the adjudicating officer has shown how overbearing he is when he made the aforesaid observations in the impugned order. He conveniently forgot that two Divisional chiefs of FII department of the Board had appreciated the difficulties which the appellant was pointing out and had even permitted it to file a modified undertaking. The aforesaid observations of the adjudicating officer also lead us to believe that there was total lack of application of mind on his part. He has referred to the "Takeover Regulations" which have no concern whatsoever with the case in hand. The aforesaid response of the adjudicating officer to the clarification sought by the appellant appears to be sheer arrogance. In this back ground, we cannot appreciate the response of the adjudicating officer and cannot but deprecate his conduct.

In the result, the appeal is allowed and the impugned order set aside. The Board is directed not to insist on the undertaking prescribed by the revised reporting format.

The appellant will have its costs which are assessed at Rs 1 lac.

Sd/-
Justice N.K. Sodhi
Presiding Officer

Sd/-
Arun Bhargava
Member

Sd/-
Utpal Bhattacharya
Member
15.5.2008
bk/-"

India's security-external, internal and economic—is far more important than the personal likes and dislikes of people in power. The nation is reeling under unprecedented recession. The people are floored by the spiraling crisis. Development is lopsided, with the rich getting richer and the poor getting poorer. The stock market, which had touched dizzy heights a year ago, has fallen by over 11,000 points in this period. Terrorism is on the rise with no monetary constraints and there are clear indications that these anti-national activities are being funded from abroad. Yet the Government of India does nothing. It is time for all right-thinking, patriotic citizens to sit up and take notice. We have to act now. Tomorrow might be too late. We might become another Colombia.

In the US, following 9/11, a law titled *Uniting and Strengthening America by Providing Appropriate Tools Required to*

Intercept and Obstruct Terrorism Act (2001) more commonly known as the *USA Patriot Act,* was enacted. The key area where tightening was done was with relation to the inflow of foreign funds. The American reasoning was that any terrorist activity requires huge funds to flourish. And if the inflow of funds dries up, the terrorism dies out or at least loses its momentum. The Federal Reserve Board (the American equivalent of the RBI) authorities minutely audited the accounts of every bank. Every investment into the country was investigated. The source of funds were traced to ascertain whether the money was legal or not.

In the United Kingdom, on March 30, 2006 the Terrorism Act was passed in the aftermath of the 7th July 2005 London bombings. This law creates new offences related to terrorism, and amends existing ones. The British Government considered the law a necessary response to an unparalleled terrorist threat, notwithstanding criticism from human rights activists.

In comparison, in India, acts of terrorism are taking place with monotonous regularity, everywhere. Practically every State in the country has experienced the phenomenon of senseless, wanton violence. Crowded trains and railway stations, bus stands, bazars, places of worship, tourist destinations, even India's Parliament House have been used by sundry terrorist outfits as their playground, often with devastating effect. So many innocent people have died. So many valiant personnel from our security forces have also perished. And what does the Indian Government do? It abrogates the *Prevention of Terrorism Act of* 2002 (POTA)! It opens the doors to unchecked entry of all sorts of funds from abroad in the name of globalization, enabling terrorist outfits from abroad to not only fund terrorism in India but to also cripple India economically. This is nothing short of economic terrorism. Much has already been said about the scrapping of POTA, and I shall not go deeper into this now. It is the open door policy for foreign funds about which I intend to elaborate.

While an Indian citizen in India has to provide his/her address proof, photo ID proof, PAN details, etc to open even an ordinary savings bank account in a local bank, foreign investors can hide their identity under a sub-account by making use of Participatory Notes to route their investments, often running into hundreds of crores. The main reason for the popularity of a P-note is in fact the anonymity it provides. P-notes are instruments issued by registered Foreign Institutional Investors (FIIs) to overseas investors who wish to invest in the Indian Stock Market without registering themselves with the market regulator—the Securities and Exchange Board of India (SEBI). Almost all top FIIs like Fidelity Investments, Merrill Lynch, Morgans Stanley and Credit Lyonnais issue P-notes, a derivative without parallel in the world.

As stated earlier, concerned about the possibility of influx of large quantities of terrorist funds into India through this route, SEBI had asked the FIIs to disclose the identities of the holders of P-notes. But there was no compliance. Surprisingly, the Finance Ministry did nothing about this. Investments through the P-notes route, are believed to be largely responsible for sudden, unexplained fluctuations in the stock-market indices, including the huge falls which have even resulted in suicides in Dalal Street. As a consequences, our Stock Markets are rigged by anti-national forces directly or indirectly.

Repeatedly pressed by patriotic persons, the Finance Ministry however has failed to answer why this special exemption to P-Notes is being provided especially when:

(i) The Tarapore Committee appointed by the Ministry had recommended that P-Notes be abolished in the national interest and in the interest of financial stability.

(ii) The National Security Adviser of the Government, M.K. Narayanan stated publicly that terrorists were making money on the Indian Stock Exchanges by using derivatives (like P-Notes).

(iii) The former SEBI Chairman Damodaran, during his tenure, had written several times that P-Notes being outside the normal disclosure rules was playing havoc with the stability of the Stock market and also leading to its manipulation. But Damodaran was given his marching orders.

(iv) A Tribunal headed by a sitting Delhi High Court Judge had, in an Order on 15.5.2008, exonerated Goldman Sachs of the charge of non-compliance of SEBI regulations on disclosure, and instead it fined the SEBI a sum of Rs.1 lakh for asking for disclosure!

The bitter truth thus is that India's corporate world's success stories are founded on fudged accounts and on undisclosed and unreported funding through black money held by corrupt politicians and notorious criminals. In 1991, the respected Swiss magazine *Schweitzer Illustrate* published the by-product revelations of the Marcos investigation: therefrom it can be seen that Sonia Gandhi had been a legatee to Rs.10,000 crores in illegal Swiss bank deposits. Originally these accounts were in names of various Nehru family members including Rajiv Gandhi. He is no more; but in February 1991 in a candid conversation with me he confided with genuine regret why and how this came about, and what he would do once he became PM again. But he was assassinated and that booty has gone to his named beneficiary and which I estimate has grown since then to Rs. 25,000 crores. Indians have about $ 1.5 trillion in Swiss banks alone, not to mention deposits in Liechtenstien, the Isle of Man, Cayman Islands, Macao etc.,etc.. All this money can be brought back by legal methods within two months, but who can cast the first stone today?

Earlier this money used to lie in the bank vaults; but now thanks to Participatory Notes [PNs] and the Mauritius route, this money is returning to India and in the BSE to earn windfall profits. Even terrorists are funding Indian corporates via the share purchases through the PNs. According to me, the BSE has become the most rigged stock market in the world after the Shanghai exchange. This money enables politicians and business persons to carry cash around the world for pleasure, and sometimes they get caught with it. For example, on September 27, 2001, Rahul Gandhi [now MP] and his girl friend were arrested by the FBI at Boston's Logan airport with $ 160,000 in cash, which had not been declared to the US Customs. US law requires cash at hand of more than $10,000 to be declared. But he was let off after nine hours in FBI custody at the intervention of the then BJP led government, which for some mysterious reason had played guardian to Ms. Sonia Gandhi and her family throughout their tenure.

With a thousand crore rupees as legal tender, (much as Rs.10 is for the middle class), politicians and criminals have entered to finance the Indian corporate world. That rotten core of our growth story is the real threat to the nation's security. Any enemy of India can thus ruin the nation by leveraging the financial web that fuels our greed for more profits and the search for short-cuts to satisfy that greed. Satyam's real truth is just that, and not the criminality and betrayal of trust by Raju. That root cause has to be addressed and removed before the nation goes under, as we did go from the height of our prosperity in 1200 AD to utter poverty in 1947. Such a depressing event can happen again if there is compliance, capitulation and conspiracy of silence to fraud. How was it possible for accountants to not know what was going on? What about the glossy business magazines and pink and costly financial newspapers which kept quiet on Dr. Sarma's complaint and Metro Rail Chief Sridharan's outrage at the Maytas fraud? They must have all known but chose to look the other way at soft targets. On whom did the 185 Fortune 500 companies which were Satyam's clients, rely for clearance? What about the 24/7 TV news channels which throw a fit by the minute on the security cover given to politicians. Why did they refuse to see this nexus? Was it their greed, or cowardice since corporates are hard targets?

The dimly visible good news is that even today the vast majority of Indians are moral and honest. Hence, the Satyams, Harshad Mehtas, and others should wake those of us up who can do something and galvanise collectively into action. Democracy and national integrity are not spectator sports like a cricket match. Nor can we be running commentators only. Each of us is a player, and has to determine what he can do for the country.

Hence, of all the frauds in India, the P-Notes cum Mauritius Treaty are the most sinister and anti-national of scams. It obviously had patronage of the Delhi establishment since neither the Congress Party, nor the Opposition want to speak about it. This collusion is at the root of the corruption in the nation.

The question that remains is: what governance principles should be adopted not only to rescue the Indian economy, from the current tail-spin, foretelling a possible enormous fiscal crisis, but also to rapidly progress to a developed corruption-minimal nation status in the next two or three decades? Hence concisely stated, for this to be achieved, the Indian economy should be founded on a harmonization of efficient organizational leadership and spiritual values. That can be nurtured only bottom up i.e., educate our growth accordingly—to synthesize material pursuits with spiritual values. Ultimately it will also be decided by how we vote in elections. But we need a new ideology to combat the cancer of corruption in our system. It is for this reasons we need to study two gigantic frauds of the 21st century in India: Satyam and Spectrum, and judge whether any "Sundaram" (beauty) is left in our development trajectory and whether we can move towards a full bloom of the "Sundaram" that foreign travelers glowing wrote about a prosperous India less than a thousand years ago.

Chapter II

Corporate Governance Concept in India

Corporate governance encompasses a commitment to ethical business conduct. It is about maximizing shareholders' dividends and value, about just executive compensation on a sustainable basis, while ensuring fairness to all the stakeholders. Stakeholders include customers, employees, investors, vendors, the government and the society-at-large. Corporate governance, therefore, is critical to enhancing and retaining investors' trust and societal confidence in the profit-oriented business model. In this context, companies that practice the highest standards of corporate governance are to be respected and rewarded. Today, on that reputation is vested the strength of a global corporation's ability to access high-quality capital, at the lowest cost, from a global pool of investors.

The recent corporate scandals and the subsequent bankruptcy of several companies, has brought into focus the need for more effective regulation of corporate affairs. However, we must bear in mind that while legislations can create checks and balances, these cannot be the cure in itself. The cure instead lies in the cultural climate of the nation—on whether pursuit of acquisition of wealth is the only norm of success, or whether there are multiple values to be harmonized by the economic players.

The board of directors is responsible for running a company but they also perform a fiduciary duty on behalf of all their stakeholders. While performing this duty, corporate governance requires that the corporation is run on ethical standards. They have to ensure that the company complies with all the laws of the land.

In the US, the Sarbanes-Oxley Act brought stricter controls on the management, accountants, lawyers, research analysts, rating agencies, etc., after the Enron scandal. Under the Act, the management of corporations is now held accountable under criminal law for the financial statements. Mis-statements can attract severe penalties and prosecution. In India government has, as usual, appointed committees to look into various aspects of corporate governance. These committees have come out with their own set of recommendations, but the legislation in place and the empowered regulators are still toothless or not enforced [1].

Table: Corporate Governance—Differences between International and Indian Codes

Shareholders' Rights		
Secure methods of ownership registration convey or transfer shares	Yes	Shares traded through a stock exchange are held in dematerialised form in the depositories. Companies must maintain a register of shareholders or outsource this function to a share transfer agent. Shares are freely transferable. Guarantee funds largely eliminate settlement risk.
Voting Rights	Yes	All shares are equal within one class. Indian companies to issue shares with multiple voting rights or dividends as long as such shares do not exceed 25 per cent of share capital and shareholders approve the issuance. Non voting preferred shares exist, but are not popular.
Institutional investors and their voting rights	No	Pension funds do not play a corporate governance role. The Unit Trust of India (UTI), the Life Insurance Company (LIC) and the General Insurance Company (GIC) are the three largest institutional investors and are government owned. Together, they own 15-20 per cent of the listed sector. These institutions seldom exercise their voting rights but exert influence through directors nominated to the board of their portfolio companies.
Proxy Voting	Yes	No notarisation required; registration 48 hours prior; no postal ballots.
Cumulative Vote/Proportional Representation	No	
Shareholder Meetings/Other Rights	Yes	The annual general meeting (AGM) be held every year, a notice convening the meeting be sent to all shareholders at least 21 days in advance of the meeting. Shareholders controlling 10 per cent of voting rights or paid-up capital to call a special or Extraordinary General Meeting (EGM), quorum at the AGM may not Sufficiently protect minority shareholders. Shareholders may inspect the minutes of the AGM.

[1] Banaji, Jairus and Gauram Mody: Corporate Governance and the Indian Prime Sector, Oxford University Press, DATE.

Minority Shareholder Protection	Yes	The legal structure for corporate governance in India provides for strong minority shareholder protection compared with other emerging markets. Clause 49 stipulates that there must be a board-level shareholder grievance committee to address such disputes, and that a non-executive director must chair this committee. In theory India's legal framework provides for strong minority shareholder protection, in practice minority shareholders cannot always garner the strength to exercise their voting rights together.
Share in the profits of the corporation	Yes	The board of directors proposes the dividend, and the AGM approves it. Dividends must be paid within 30 days. As for complaints about transfer of shares and non-receipt of dividends while the redress rate has been an impressive 95 per cent, there were still over 1,35,000 complaints pending with the SEBI.
Take-over Code	Yes	Increasing takeover activity.
Insider Tracing and Self-Dealing Prohibition	Yes	Criminal offence, but difficult to monitor due to multiple listings.
Pre-emptive Rights	Yes	
Changes in firm capital structure	Yes	Acquisition of more than 15 per cent of shares or voting rights requires the acquirer to make a public offering. To approve a merger, under SEBI's regulations a shareholder vote of 75 per cent is required. New capital issues first be offered to existing shareholders in proportion to their shares of paid-up capital.
Stakeholders rights	Yes	The corporate governance framework requires the board of directors to discuss material issues regarding employees and other stakeholders. Civil courts discourage creditors from litigating on issues relating to governance, citing "indoor management" policy. Promoters are not eligible for stock options. There is no ceiling on how many stock options can be issued. The options are tied to specific performance goals and vested over a time period - typically three to six years. The quality of the information varies markedly between the first two hundred listed companies and the rest of the market.
Oversight of Management		
Board Structure Independent Directors	No	Mandatory for large companies as of March 2001 and for most small companies in 2003: If chairman is also CEO, $\geq$ 50 per cent; if not, $\geq$30 per cent. Despite the requirement for board independence, the availability of trained independent directors in India is limited.
Board Meetings	No	The board should meet at least four times a year, board quorum only requires that 33 per cent of board members or two members, whichever is greater, be present. There is no provision that specifies whether non-executive or independent members need be present.
Nomination and Election of Directors	No	Founder/promoters or controlling shareholders generally appoint directors. There is limited scope for minority shareholders to recommend director nominees.
Committee Practices	No	Mandatory for large companies as of March 2001 and for most small companies in 2003.

Disclosure and Transparency		
External Auditors	Yes	Annual statements audited. Auditors appointed/removed at AGM.
Consolidated Statements	No	If ownership interest ≥50 per cent abridged data mandatory in annual report.
Segment Reporting	No	Expected to be implemented soon.
Disclosure of Price Sensitive Information	Yes	To the correspondent stock exchange and SEBI. SEBI's Insider Trading Regulations, 2002, require every company to appoint a compliance officer who is responsible for setting policies, procedures, and monitoring adherence to the rules for the preservation of "price sensitive information" to prevent insider trading. There is no good legal definition of insider trading, which hampers surveillance efforts.
Other Responsibilities	No	No provisions in the Indian governance framework for a investor relations programme and to provide a policy statement concerning environmental issues and social responsibility.
Audit Committee	Yes	Minimum of three directors as members, with at least two-thirds of the members being independent. Clause 49 does not prohibit the contemporaneous provision of audit and non-audit services from the same entity.
Accounting-Standards and Enforcement	Yes	ICAI[23] sets out standards monitored by SEBI and ICAI. Not in full compliance with IAS.[24]
Company Officers related Disclosures	Yes	Aggregated remuneration info is required in annual report. In 2001, breakdown of remuneration by director must be provided.
Related Party Transactions	Yes	Clause 49 requires listed companies to disclose materially significant related-party transactions in the Report on Corporate Governance in the annual report to shareholders, however, it does not define the term "materially significant."
Disclosure of Ownership	Yes	To SEBI and stock exchanges when ownership crosses 5 per cent.
Risk Management and other Disclosures		The law prescribes that companies have to be rated by approved credit rating agencies before issuing securities.
Regulatory Environment[25]	Yes	The weak enforcement mechanism in the country is a key concern.

Sources: World Bank and IIF Report, 2006.
From: *Economic and Political Weekly,* September 30, 2006.

CORPORATE GOVERNANCE: THE U.S. AND INDIA

- Current Developments: legislation in both countries—SOX, Clause 49
- Motivation for legislation

U.S.	India
Scandals	Attract "patient" capital Attract foreign investment Asian currency crisis International lending bodies

SARBOX VS. CLAUSE 49

A. Shareholder Rights—U.S.	Shareholder Rights—India
Multiple classes of shareholders	One share, one vote, but warrants
Dividents—discretionary with Board of Directos	Dividents approved by shareholders at the AGM
Lack of shareholder approval for director/management compensation	Required shareholder approval
	Grievance committee for shareholders
B. Board Independence—U.S.	Board Independence—India
At least 51 percent	Two-tier system—generally independent
	Stated criteria for independence
	Maximum number of committees and chairmanships
	Loss of independence—9 years
	Required code of ethics
C. Audit Committees—U.S.	Audit Committees—India
Majority independent	2/3 independent
Financial literacy	Financial literacy at least one should have finance experience
Review Financial Internal Controls	Broad powers—review financial and non-financial controls—minimum 4 meetings per annum
Must meet separately from management	
Required independent compensation committee	
D. Responsibility of the officers—U.S.	Responsibility of the officers—India
CEO and CFO certification	CEO and CFO certification, 40 year history under CA
	Risk Management policy disclosed
	CEO/CFO certify—compliance with all laws
	Corp Gov. reports quarterly
Whistleblower protection required	
	SBUs must share one director

E. Penalties—U.S.	Penalties—India
Criminal and civil penalties for individuals and companies	
Personal liability for financial restatements	
	Initially: Delisting
	Currently: also financial penalties
F. Interpretation and Implementation—U.S.	Interpretation and Implementation—India
Judicial system active	Judicial system overburdened
Creditor rights highly protected	Creditor rights: legal, but overburdened courts
	Noncompliance: big issue
	PSUs and SEBI
	Required phased implementation by size
	Regulatory arbitrage: SEBI, DCA, Exchanges

Source: Perspectives on Corporate Governance: A Case Study of U.S. and India a study by [Lal C. Chugh, Joseph W. Meador and Professors of Finance, University of Massachusetts, Boston and Northeastern University, respectively].

Of the many committees appointed by government, The Naresh Chandra Committee's report on Corporate Audit and Government and an Interim Report on Corporate Governance by Shri Narayana Murthy of Infosys are worthy of note.

The role and responsibilities of a director of a company are crucial factors in corporate governance. A company is, by itself a 'legal person', having a continuous existence, independent of the existences of its members. However, it is an artificial person and can, of necessity, act only through the agency of natural persons. A company has no mind of its own and directors represent the directing mind and the will of the company.

In a remarkable piece of elucidation of directors/company relationship, the Supreme Court in Life Insurance Corporation of India v. Escorts Ltd. {(1986) 59 Comp Cas 548}, pronounced as follows [2]:

"A company is in some respects an institution like a state functioning under its "basic constitution," consisting of the Companies Act and the Memorandum of Association." The members in general meeting and the directorate are described as the two primary organs of a company, comparable with the legislative and the executive organs of a parliamentary democracy, where the legislative sovereignty rests with the parliament, while the administration is left to the executive government, subject to a measure of control by parliament through its power to force a change of government. Like the government, the directors will be answerable to "parliament" constituted by the general meeting."

As per the Companies Act, it is mandatory for a company to have directors. No company is exempt from this requirement.

In a legal sense, a "Director" performs according to the Companies Act, the company's Memorandum and Articles of Association and the share holders of the company.

A Director is an officer of the company (section 2(30)) and an "officer who is in default" (Sections 2(31) and 5) for purpose of certain contraventions of the Companies Act, 1956.

All the directors are collectively referred to as the "Board of Directors" or "Board" (Section 2(6)).

A director may be a full time working director, namely managing or whole time director, covered by a service contract. Managing and whole time directors are in charge of the day to day conduct of the affairs of a company and are together with other

[2] Rajagopalan, R: *Directors and Corporate Governance,* Company Law Institute of India Pvt. Ltd. Chennai, 2003.

team members collectively known as the "management" of the company.

On the other hand, a non-executive director has nothing to do with day to day management of the company and he attends board meetings and meetings of the committees of the board of which he is a member.

There is another category of directors, who are *deemed* to be directors, while they are not appointed as such. Such a director is also referred to as "Shadow director," who derives the deemed status by virtue of his giving instructions (other than professional advices) according to which "appointed" directors are accustomed to act. Certain provisions of the Companies Act apply to "Shadow directors" as if they are "appointed" directors.

LEGAL POSITION AND DUTIES OF A DIRECTOR

The legal position as well as the duties of a director have been clearly expounded in the Report of the High Powered Expert Committee on Companies and MRTP Acts, 1978, as follows:

> "Directors are appointed to act in the interests of the company and an important area of their legal responsibility stems from the law of trusts—they have a fiduciary relationship with the company. The duties arising from the relationship are well defined viz. to exercise their powers for the benefit of the company, to avoid a conflict of interests and a duty not to restrict their right (by contract or otherwise) to freely and fully exercise their duties and powers.
>
> In addition to their fiduciary duties, directors also owe a duty of care to the company, not to act negligently in the management of its affairs, the standard being that of a reasonable man looking after his own affairs."

A company on incorporation has its own independent identity distinct from that of its members. It is said that a company thus wears the veil of corporate personality. However, in certain situations, through the principle of "Lifting the Corporate Veil" the courts do try to look behind this legal structure to discover the realities and ignore the corporate personality to bring to book the human beings behind the veil.

Thus the Sir Adrian Cadbury Committee, which went into corporate governance issues in U.K., defines corporate governance, "as the system by which companies are directed and controlled. The basic objective of corporate governance is to enhance and maximize shareholder value and protect the interest of other stake holders."

Mr. Alan Greenspan, the former U.S. Federal Reserve Board Chairman, puts it very appropriately as follows:

> "Corporate Governance has evolved over the past century, to more effectively promote the allocation of nation's savings to its most productive uses and the resulting structure of business incentives, reporting and accountability has served us well.... Yet our most recent experiences with the bankruptcies of companies and preceding that several lesser such incidents suggest that the governance of our companies has strayed from our perceptions of how it is supposed to work. By law, shareholders own corporations and ideally, corporate managers should be working on behalf of shareholders to allocate business resources to their optimum use."

CORPORATE GOVERNANCE IN INDIA

Corporate governance was not in the agenda of Indian companies until early 1990s. One would not find any reference till then to this subject in any book of law or even management studies.

Thus, in India, although weaknesses in the system—such as undesirable stock market practices, boards of directors without adequate fiduciary responsibilities, poor disclosure practices, lack of transparency and crony capitalism—were crying for reforms and improved governance, there was no real push. The momentum gathered albeit slowly, once the economy was opening up and the liberalization processes got initiated.

The Securities and Exchange Board of India (SEBI) appointed a committee on corporate governance on May 7, 1999, with eighteen members under the Chairmanship of Shri Kumaramangalam Birla to promote and raise the standards of corporate governance. The report of the committee was approved by SEBI at its meeting held on 25.1.2000. Below is a summary of the Report's Mandatory Recommendations:

1. Applicability

   Applicable to all listed companies with paid-up share capital of Rs. 3 crore and above.

2. Board of directions

   The Board of Directors of a company must have an optimum combination of executive and non-executive Directors with not less than 50% of the Board comprising of non-executive Chairman and at least half of the Board in case the company has an executive Chairman.

   The Committee defines independent directors as directors who apart from receiving director's remuneration do not have any material pecuniary relationship or transactions with the company, its promoters, its management or its subsidiaries, which in judgment of the board may affect independence of judgment of the director.

3. Audit Committee

   A qualified and independent Audit Committee should be set

up to enhance the credibility of the financial disclosures and to promote transparency.

The Audit Committee should have minimum 3 members, all being non-executive directors, with majority being independent, and at least one Director having Financial and Accounting knowledge.

The Chairman should be an independent Director and must be present at the Annual General Meetings to answer Shareholders queries.

Audit Committee specifically functions as the bridge between the Board, the Statutory auditors and the internal auditors.

Full disclosure of the Remuneration package of all the directors covering salary, benefits, bonuses, stock options, pension, fixed component, performance linked incentives along with the performance criteria, service contracts, notice period.

Severance fees, etc. to be made in the section on corporate governance of the annual report.

The SEBI Board considered and adopted in its meeting held on January 25, 2000, the recommendations of the Committee on Corporate Governance.

In accordance with the guidelines provided by the SEBI the market regulator, the stock exchanges in India have modified the requirements by incorporating in the listing-agreement a new Clause 49, so that proper disclosure for corporate governance is made by the companies.

A separate section on Corporate Governance in the annual reports therefore has to be introduced covering brief statement on Company's philosophy on code of governance, Board of Directors, Audit Committee, Remuneration Committee, Shareholders

Committee, General Body Meetings, Disclosures, Means of communication, General shareholder information.

The Naresh Chandra Committee was constituted on August 21, 2002, by the Ministry of Finance and Company Affairs to address issues relating to corporate Governance and to examine the Auditor-Company relationship and to regulate the role of auditors. The trigger was the happenings in the U.S. and certain instances in India involving auditors. In fact, the spontaneity with which the U.S. responded to the high profile corporate scams by enacting the Sarbanes-Oxley Act in a very short time, to take strong measures to deter recurrences of such scams, had made the Indian regulators and authorities to come out with a similar response.

The Committee submitted its report to the Finance Ministry on December 23, 2002. Commenting on the prevailing scenario, the Committee has reported on the poor structure and composition of boards of directors of Indian companies, scant fiduciary responsibility, poor disclosures and transparency, inadequate accounting and auditing standards, the need for experts to go through thoroughly the nitty-gritty of transactions among companies, banks and financial institutions, capital markets, etc. The Committee has been remarkably candid in highlighting that in India companies need to follow very stringent guidelines on Corporate governance and that there is a wide gap between prescription and practice. The Committee pinpointed that the defaulters escape the adverse legal consequences, as the involved processes almost always get caught in the web of inefficiency, corruption and the intricate, dilatory legal system. Thus, *while Corporate Governance reforms in India far outstrip those of many other countries, in the matter of performance the country is very much lagging behind.*

The Committee recognized the independence of audit as one of the key factors of governance and recommended suitable measures for the prohibition of direct financial interest in the audit client by the audit firms, its partners or members of the engagement team as well as their direct relatives.

The Committee recommended that the auditors before agreeing to be appointed, should provide certificates of independence to the audit committee or the board of directors of the client company.

Importantly with regard to disclosure requirements, the Committee recommended that the auditors should disclose implications of contingent liabilities, so that the investors and shareholders have a clear picture of a company's contingent liabilities. The management on its part should provide a clear description of each material liability and its risks and the auditors should give their comments on management's views, in clear terms.

In addition to the existing provisions in the Companies Act, regarding qualifications averred in audit reports, the Committee has made further recommendations to the effect that the auditor should read out the qualifications with explanations, to the shareholders at the company's annual general meeting and the audit firm is mandated to send separately a copy of the qualified report to the Registrar of Companies, SEBI and the Principal Stock Exchange, with a copy of the letter to the management of the company.

A very significant recommendation of the Committee is to require a company to furnish a certificate by the CEO and the CFO stating that the signing officers have reviewed the balance sheet, profit and loss account and all schedules and notes on accounts as well as the cash flow statement and the directors' report, that the statements do not contain any materially untrue or misleading statement, not omitted any material fact, that the statements present a true and fair picture of the financial and operational state of the company and that the signing officers are responsible for establishing and maintaining internal controls. But there is no serious criminal penalty on the CEO and CFO for failure to do so.

The Committee recommended that in the event of any materially significant mis-statements or omissions, the signing officers will return to the company that part of any bonus or incentive or equity based compensation which was inflated on account of such errors, as decided by the audit committee. The punishment part thus is not commensurate with the severity of the offence. While the R.D. Joshi's Committee had recommended imprisonment for those providing incorrect financial statements, for a period up to 10 years, the existing provisions under Section 211 of the Companies Act carry a penalty of only six months imprisonment.

To give effect to the recommendations of Shri N.R. Narayana Murthy Committee on Corporate Governance, SEBI approved modifications in Clause 49 of the listing agreement in a circular dated August 26, 2003. All companies are now required to comply with the provisions of revised clause 49, effective April 1, 2004. The Committee on Financial Sector Assessment had also endorsed this in its Report released on March 30, 2009.

No discussion on corporate governance is complete without addressing the issue of "whistle blowing." "Whistle blowing" is an act by which an employee in an organization makes public announcements of incidents of mal-practices within the organization or otherwise perpetrated by the organization. Usually, this happens when the person "blowing the whistle" does not get response from within the organization to check or stop the practices in question. The whistle blower is at great personal risk of losing his/her job or being punished otherwise by the affected persons in authority. In the U.S. the regulators have recognized the great role of whistle blowers in tracking high profile scandals in large organizations, which would have otherwise not come out. In fact, women employees not highly placed in the organizations stood out in their extraordinary efforts. Naturally, the question of protection of whistle blowers came up at the highest levels among regulators and commensurate provisions have been incorporated in the SOX Act, 2002.

2.3 *Sarbanes-Oxley Act, 2002 of USA*

Regulator Response...
The Sarbanes-Oxley Act (SOX Act) is a serious attempt to address all the issues associated with corporate failures to achieve quality governance and to restore investors confidence.

Important provisions contained in the SOX Act are briefly given below:

Establishment of Public Company Accounting Oversight Board (PCAOB)

The SOX Act creates a new board consisting of five members of whom only two will be certified Public Accountants. All accounting firms will have to register themselves with this board and submit among other details, particulars of fees received from Public Company clients for audit and non-audit services, financial information about the firm, list of firms' staff who participate in audits, quality control policies, information on civil, criminal and disciplinary proceedings against the firm or any of the staff. The board will conduct annual inspections of firms which audit more than 100 public companies and once in three years in other cases. The board will establish rules governing audit, quality control, ethics, independence and other standards. It can conduct investigations and disciplinary proceedings and can impose sanctions on auditors.

The board reports to SEC. The board is required to send its report to SEC annually, which report will then be forwarded by SEC to the Congress.

The new board replaces the old one which was funded by accounting firms and was not effective. The new board is funded by fees collected from public companies based on their market capitalisation.

Audit Committee

The SOX Act provides for a "new improved" Audit Committee. The members of the Committee are drawn from among the directors of the board of the company but should all be independent directors, as defined in the Act.

The audit committee is responsible for appointment, fixing of fees and overseeing of the work of independent auditors. The committee is also responsible for establishing, reviewing the procedures for the receipt, treatment of accounts, internal control and audit complaints received by the company from the interested or affected parties.

The SOX Act requires that registered Public Accounting firms should report directly to the audit committee on all critical accounting policies and practices and other related matters.

Conflict of Interest

Public Accounting firms should not perform any audit service for a Publicly traded company, if CEO, CFO, Controller, Chief Accounts Officer or any person serving in an equivalent position was employed by such firm and participated in any capacity in the audit of that company during the one year period preceding the date of the initiation of the audit.

Audit Partner Rotation

The SOX Act provides for mandatory rotation of lead audit partner as well as partner reviewing audit every five years.

Prohibition of Non-audit Services

Under the SOX Act, auditors are prohibited from providing non-audit services concurrently with audit/financial review services. Non-audit services include book-keeping, financial and information system design, internal audit, human resource development services, investment advice, investment banking services, legal advice, appraisal, valuation and actuarial services.

Limited permitted non-audit services such as tax advice are to be pre-approved by the Audit Committee.

CEO and CFOs Required to Affirm Financials

Chief Executive Officers and Chief Finance Officers are required to certify the reports filed with the Securities Exchange Commission. If the financials are required to be restated, due to material non-compliance, "as a result of misconduct" of CEO or CFO, then such CEO or CFO will have to return to the company bonus and any other incentives received by them. This applies to equity-based compensation received during the first 12 months after initial public offering. False and/or improper certifications can attract fine ranging from $ 1 Million to $ 5 Million or up to 10 years imprisonment or both.

Loans to Directors

The SOX Act prohibits U.S. and foreign companies with securities traded within U.S. from making or arranging from third parties any type of personal loan to directors. It appears that the existing loans are not affected, but material modifications or renewal of loans and arrangements of existing loans are banned.

Attorneys

The attorneys dealing with the publicly traded companies are required to report evidence of material violation of securities law or breach of fiduciary duty or similar violations by the company or any agent of the company to the Chief Counselor CEO and if the Counselor CEO does not appropriately respond to the evidence, the attorney must report the evidence to the audit committee or the board of directors.

Securities Analysts

The SOX Act provides that brokers and dealers of securities should not retaliate or threaten to retaliate against an analyst employed by the broker or dealer for any adverse, negative or unfavourable research report on a Public Company. The Act further provides for disclosure of conflict of interest by the securities analysts and brokers or dealers in the following cases:

(a) whether the analyst has investments or debt in the, company he is reporting on
(b) whether any compensation received by the broker, dealer or analyst is "appropriate in the public interest and consistent with the protection of investors."
(c) whether the company (issuer) has been a client of the broker or dealer and
(d) whether the analyst received compensation with respect to a research report based on investment banking revenues.

Penalties

The penalties prescribed under the SOX Act for any wrong doings are very stiff. Penalties for wilful violations are even stiffer. Any CEO or CFO providing a certificate knowing that the certificate does not meet with the criteria stated, may be fined up to $ 1 million and or imprisonment up to 10 years. However, those who "wilfully" provide certification knowing that the certificate does not meet the required criteria, can be punished with a fine of $ 5 million and/or with a prison term up to 20 years. These heavy penalties are bound to be a deterrent for wrong doers. In contrast, the Indian situation is quite different, and corporate crimes are hardly dealt with an iron hand. It is high time that the Indian regulators catch up.

Very importantly, the SOX Act provides for studies to be conducted by the Securities Exchange Commission or the Government Accounting office in the following areas:

(1) Auditors Rotation
(2) Off-Balance Sheet transactions
(3) Consolidation of accounting firms and its impact on the accounting industry.
(4) Role of Credit Rating Agencies
(5) Study of violators and violations during the years 1998-2001
(6) SEC enforcement actions in the past five years.
(7) Role of investment banks and financial advisers and
(8) "Principle-based" accounting

Thus the sweeping provisions towards protection of the whistle blowers include, imprisonment up to 10 years of anyone retaliating against a corporate whistle blower. The Department of Labor (DOL), the US equivalent of the Ministry of Labour, is directed to complete its adjudication of whistle blowers' cases within 180 days, failing which, the whistle blower may either elect to stay with DOL or seek *de novo* trial in court. The whistle blowers are allowed to seek redressals including reinstatement, back-pay with interest, compensatory damages, special damages, attorney fees and costs. Similar provisions do exist in the U.K. also.

The Insider Trading Regulations issued by SEBI in 1992 have now been amended and the new regulations were notified during February, 2002, viz., the SEBI (Insider Trading) (Amendment) (Regulation) 2002, to remove the shortcomings found in the earlier regulations and also to make them more effective. This will protect investors' interest and ensure transparency in dealings of securities of companies by employees, directors, officers and other market intermediaries. SEBI has further amended these regulations during November, 2002 with the introduction of the SEBI (Prohibition of Insider Trading) (Second Amendment) Regulations, 2002.

The Insider Trading Regulations shall be applicable to those persons who have temporary or permanent relationship with the company including its directors, officers, designated employees, professionals, businessmen and their dependent relatives, who may reasonably be expected to have an access to unpublished price sensitive information in relation to that company.

As per the regulation 3, no insider shall—

(i) either on his own behalf or on behalf of any other person, deal in securities of a company listed on any stock exchange when in possession of any unpublished price sensitive information; or

(ii) communicate, counsel or procure, directly or indirectly, any unpublished price sensitive information to any person, who, while in possession of such unpublished price sensitive information, shall not deal in securities;

Provided that nothing contained above, shall be applicable to any communication required in the ordinary course of business or profession or employment or under any law.

We shall apply these concepts to see where corporate India has gone wrong judged by two illustrative frauds, one in the private sector namely Satyam Computer Services Ltd and the other in the public or government owned sector, the Telecom of the Ministry of Information Technology in the allocation of spectrum for mobile phone services.

ACCOUNTING AND ANALYSIS

Accounts, traditionally, were meant to be statements of cash-in and cash-out. Accountants worldwide appear to be changing all that? The balance sheet reflected cash-in and cash-out on capital account (to be reflected in the profit and loss account over a number of years, through depreciation or amortisation). The profit and loss account was expected to be a statement of revenue surplus or deficit over revenue expenditure, and at best a statement that also reflected profit or loss on sale of fixed assets.

Instead Notional accounting is now in, which is not necessarily a statement of cash movements. It is, often, the management's/auditor's *perception* of business' value.

A number of items, which should really be part of the main accounts, are seen as "contingent liabilities." For instance, bills discounted and loans assigned to others are shown as part of contingencies, although the ultimate liability remains with the borrowing company. The question that arises is, "Are annual published accounts really a statement of accounts or a presentation of analysis?"

AN ANALYST'S APPROACH

An analyst's viewpoint could differ from an accountant's approach. The treatment of each item in the accounts could depend on the purpose for which the analysis is being done. For example, deferred tax may be of greater significance to a lender because in the event of a winding up, a company may actually be required to pay the deferred tax. Deferred tax would concern an equity shareholder to the extent that distributable profits are reduced. Thus it may be a good idea to show notional provisions in an analysis form at the end of audited accounts, rather than make them an integral part of the accounts. This would ensure that the main accounts retain the original form and truly reflect actual cash movements.

Accounting standards prescribe guidelines as well as rules for accounting but occasionally, personnel judgment is required while drawing up the accounts. There are gray areas in the accounting of inflows and outflows and we may need to make choices between classification of an inflow as an income or a liability, an outflow as an expense on an asset. Even after making a choice, which is not always easy, there are issues of classifying an item as a "current" or "non-current" asset or liability. Again, individual analysts may differ in their perceptions. Reclassifications can alter results and ratios dramatically.

A few examples from CRISIL's reclassifications, based on financial statements of Indian manufacturing companies are given below. Their sample size covers 616 companies, including 375 companies that form part of the "A" Group of The Stock Exchange, Mumbai and the S&P CNX 500. We have reworked ratios and numbers of the entire database to look at possible effects of adopting different classifications. An accounting approach used by a single company, which if applied by all other companies, could change the entire look and feel of aggregate corporate financial numbers!

Contingent liabilities are an integral part of annual reports and could be of a different type. Contingencies such as "capital expenditure yet to be incurred" or "lease rentals yet to be paid" are not really contingent upon any other event. These contingencies commit future expenses under planned capital expenditure and could be excluded from the list contingencies.

Other forms of contingent liability could be, inter alia:

- Guarantees/counter guarantees given by the company to bankers
- Claims against company not acknowledged as debt by the company
- Disputed demands raised by octroi, income tax, excise, customs and sales tax authorities
- Disputed matters pending in the High Court or Supreme Court
- Damages claimed by customers for a job undertaken by a company
- Export obligation arising out of import of plant and machinery awaiting approval from government

- Investment held in an affiliate company pledged with lenders for securing financial assistance to the affiliate company

The table below gives the list of top ten companies, which had the highest contingencies excluding capital expenditure yet to be incurred and lease rentals yet to be paid, as a percentage of tangible net worth:

Table 1: Contingent Liabilities Ratios: 2002

Rs. in crores

Sr. No.	Company	Year ending	Total Contingent Liabilities	Tangible Net Worth (TNW)	Contingent Liabilities as % of TNW
1	DGP Windsor (India) Ltd	30 Jun 02	24.94	0.27	9237.04
2	Ispat Industries Ltd	31 Mar 02	3008.24	271.64	1107.44
3	Simplex Mills Co. Ltd	31 Mar 02	33.50	4.04	829.21
4	Jindal Vijayanagar Steel Ltd	31 Mar 02	677.17	122.50	552.21
5	Andrew Yule & Co Ltd	31 Mar 02	127.92	-18.36	-696.73
6	GTC Industries Ltd	31 Mar 02	588.21	-79.62	-738.77
7	Mysore Cements Ltd	31 Mar 02	53.75	-4.43	-1213.32
8	Glofame Cotspon Industries Ltd	31 Mar 02	202.91	-15.10	-1343.77
9	Amtrex Hitachi Appliances Ltd	30 Sep 02	21.16	-1.45	-1459.31
10	Orient Paper & Industries Ltd	31 Mar 02	85.54	-3.03	-2823.10

Source: Global Data Services of India Ltd

Thus we see, contingent liabilities which do not show up in the profit/loss accounts can be as high as 9237% of tangible networth!

Traditionally, "bills discounted" are reported as contingent liabilities, although they are equivalent to loans against bills or loans against debtors. The original borrower remains the final recourse to the lender. Analysts often add back discounted bills to bank borrowings (on the liabilities side) and to debtors (on the assets side). This gives a truer picture of the current ratio.

Our study shows that in aggregate analysis of all companies put together, variation in current ratio, consequent to the addition of bills discounted, is marginal and lost in the rounding off process:

Year ended March 31,	2002	2001	2000	1999	1998
Bills Discounted as % of Gross Sales	0.62%	0.58%	0.73%	0.92%	0.92%
Bills Discounted as % of Total Debtors (including bills discounted)	6.37%.	6.40%	7.08%	7.95%	7.16%
Current Ratio without Bills Discounted	1.0	1.1	1.1	1.1	1.2
Current Ratio with Bills Discounted	1.0	1.1	1.1	1.1	1.2
Bills Discounted as % of Tangible Net worth	1.59%	1.64%	1.91%	2.03%	1.91%
Bills Discounted as % of total debt (including bills discounted)	2.14%	1.95%	2.21%	2.22%	1.99%

In individual cases, however, there are wide variations. The top ten companies, which would benefit if bills discounted were not considered in the current ratio, are:

Table 2

Sr. No.	Company	Year ending	Current Ratiom (A)	Current Ratio without Bills Discourt-ing (B)	Difference (B) – (A)
1	Himatsingka Seide Ltd	30 Jun 02	7.02	8.56	1.54
2	S B & T International Ltd	31 Mar 02	2.25	3.36	1.11
3	Zodiac-jrd-mkj Ltd	31 Mar 02	100.70	101.77	1.07
4	Orchid Chemicals & Pharmaceuticals Ltd	31 Mar 02	1.73	2.37	0.64
5	Gujarat Fluorochemicals Ltd	31 Mar 02	6.85	7.43	0.58
6	Computech International Ltd	31 Mar 02	2.34	2.77	0.43
7	Krebs Biochemicals Ltd	31 Mar 02	2.65	3.06	0.41
8	Wellwin Industry Ltd	31 Sep 02	4.68	5.03	0.35
9	Ingersoll Rand (India) Ltd	30 Mar 02	3.04	3.33	0.29
10	Ipca Laboratories Ltd	31 Mar 02	2.52	2.79	0.27

Note: Advance tax is considered net of provision for tax for the purpose of calculating current ratio.

Similiarly, guarantees given on behalf of subsidiaries and affiliates can be substantial. The ultimate liability and risk on a company should be gauged by consolidating accounts of the borrower and the guarantor. This may not always be possible because details of the borrowing company on whose behalf the guarantees have been given are not available. Such details are readily available only if the borrower is a subsidiary. For example, Gammon India Ltd. had outstanding guarantees on behalf of its subsidiary aggregating Rs.515.89 crore which constituted 401.11% of its own net worth as at March 31, 2002.

Table 3

Rs. in crores

Sr. No.	Company	Year ending	Current Ratiom (A)	Current Ratio without Bills Dis-courting (B)	Difference (B) – (A)
1	Gammon (India) Ltd	31 Mar 02	128.61	515.89	401.13
2	Ispat Industires ltd	31 Mar 02	271.64	983.96	362.23
3	United Breweries Ltd (Post Demerger)	31 Mar 02	27.46	92.59	337.18
4	Jindal Iron & Steel Co Ltd	31 Mar 02	286.70	695.99	242.76
5	Shyam Telecom Ltd	31 Mar 02	206.58	347.20	168.07
6	Bharat Forge Ltd	31 Mar 02	145.38	239.56	164.78
7	Adani Exports Ltd	31 Mar 02	499.43	807.22	161.63
8	United Phosphorous Ltd	31 Mar 02	438.46	582.49	132.85
9	Orient Paper & Industries Ltd	30 Mar 02	-3.03	7.91	-261.06
10	Glofame Cotspin Industries Ltd	31 Mar 02	-15.10	196.27	-1299.80

Increasingly, a number of companies have assigned their own debt to others. However, the liability on the original borrower continues to exist, since lenders do not absolve the original borrower of the responsibility to repay. While the borrowing company may assign its outstanding debt to another party, lenders are not willing to recognize the transaction. Even when debt is securitised, the onus on the original borrower does not change, although the lender could change.

Over the years, Larsen and Toubro has been assigning its outstanding debt to its subsidiary. The difference between the outstanding loan amount and the transfer value has been shown as income for the year in the books of Larsen and Toubro. Thus, the .profits of Larsen and Toubro were higher during the last three years by the following amounts:

Rs. in crore

For the year	Profit without Loan Assignment (A)	Profit through Loan Assignment (A)	Reported Profit (A) + (B)
1999-2000	288	52	340
2000-2001	264	50	314
2001-2002	333	40	373
Total	885	142	1027

Larsen and Toubro assigned the loan to its subsidiary at a value lower than the outstanding amount in its own books. The difference between the two was shown as income. Liability for repayment of the loan remains with Larsen and Toubro. There is considerable risk in recognizing this as an acceptable accounting practice. By the process of accounting, Larsen and Toubro has, in fact, converted part of its loan into income that might well be distributed as dividend. In that case, there could be problems in meeting the loan repayment obligation if the subsidiary does not have a strong financial position.

A common practice is to show sales tax deferral (repayable after twelve years) as a long-term liability at its present value and transfer the balance to income for the year. Some companies go a step further and assign the present value to another party so that the outstanding debt ceases to exist in the balance sheet. The only remaining evidence of the loan is as part of contingent liabilities. Reliance Industries is an example.

Some states in India permit prepayment of the sales tax loan on the very day that the loan gets debited to the account of the company. In the event a company prepays the amount on the day it receives the loan, then the amount prepaid is the discounted present value, as determined by the concerned authority. In that case, no contingent liability is created and it would be entirely correct to show the balance of the facility (actual loan less the amount repaid) as income. This income would be a genuine cash inflow without encumbrances. The question is, should the entire income be taken into the profit and loss account in a single year or be spread over the original life of the loan? Bharat Forge has spread the income over the life of the loan. Larsen and Toubro, on the other hand, has taken credit in a single year.

There are differing views on assignment of debt. One justification for accepting assignment of a loan as equal to transfer of a loan is that the cash out flow of the original borrower in subsequent years is reduced. However, it could well be that the company to which the loan has been assigned has weak financials and may not be able to honour the repayment obligations. It would be useful to combine the cash flows of the assignee and assignor companies to assess the true loan paying capacity.

Disputed amounts with tax authorities can be substantial and continue to remain in the notes for years. There is no study to substantiate the final outcome of these disputed amounts.

In essence, it is important to remember that contingent liabilities are sometimes not contingent at all but real liabilities.

Thus, accounts have become an instrument of public relations rather than a financial health report. How much can be hidden, and how much revealed has been the cause of the eruption of financial scandals. This is where we should begin to stem the rot in India's corporate world. Price Waterhouse Cooper (PWC) is an example of accounting irresponsibility that facilitated the Satyam Fraud.

Price Waterhouse Cooper (PWC) has come under international censure for its role or "lack of concern" in and about the Satyam fraud. In a US Court, it was alleged:

> "PWC's unqualified opinions of Satyam's financial statements were materially false and misleading ... as an accounting expert which consented to the use of its unqualified audit opinions, PWC is liable for the material misrepresentations or omissions...."

[*Excerpt* from a Class Action Complaint against Satyam, and Price Waterhouse filed in a District Court in California, US].

After Price Waterhouse Coopers' (PWC) apparent acquiescence in the Rs. 7,000 crore Satyam fraud, the revelations dragged in three others—that make up the global Big Four: Ernst and Young (EY), Deloitte, and KPMG—of the accounting world, as Table below shows:

FIRM	REVENUES ($ BILLION)	EMPLOYEES
PWC	28.2	146,700
Deloitte	27.4	165,700
EY	24.5	135,000
KPMG	22.7	137,000

Revenue figures are for the financial year ended March 2008 for PwC and Deloitte, June 2008 for EY and September 2008 for KPMG

The big four accounting firms are actually hundreds of firms held together with the glue of knowledge, economics and brand, and greed, or so it seems. They operate under an umbrella brand and a global company that promotes the brand, and researches and coordinates between the member firms (as they are usually known). EY and PWC have their coordinating firm in the UK, while Deloitte and KPMG have their coordinating companies in Switzerland. There are no cross-holdings, and ownership is always with the local seniors.

These firms or companies—as the structure may be—are owned by partners who become co-owners or shareholders as they go on to become senior members of the organization. These are largely unlimited liability partnerships and even if some of the firms are limited liability companies, the senior members who become shareholders are still designated as partners.

Globally, the Big Four rake in almost $100 billion in revenues and employ close to 5.8 lakh people. In India they are minuscule their revenue being less than $1 billion (around Rs.3,500 crore) and they employ around 21,000 people.

Other than access to methodologies, training and quality standards, the Indian affiliates get access to the firm's global clients when they do business in India. However, the One Firm concept becomes a double-edged sword when a local affiliate is pulled up for accounting wrongdoings. For instance, PWC will have to face the heat in the US because of its Indian firm's involvement in the Satyam fraud (because Satyam is listed on the New York Stock Exchange, therefore this opens it to a string of Class Action Suits).

The rules in India (revised in the Mid-1980s with an eye on the World Trade Organization (WTO) negotiations on opening up of services), do not permit the Big Four—or any multinational audit or accounting firm—to be registered in India as auditors but they can be registered in India as management consultants; PWC registered two firms as Price Waterhouse (PW) and Price Waterhouse and Co, back in the pre-Independence era and Deloitte had registered one firm under the name of Deloitte Haskins and Sells in 1978 before these rules came into force. That may explain why the audit business of the Big Four is smaller than the rest of their other operations—advisory, corporate finance and tax.

Audit (assurance in accounting jargon) is conducted by local audit firms who are part of the respective networks of the Big Four (for example, S.R. Batliboi does it for EY, A.F. Ferguson and C.C. Choksi for Deloitte, BSR for KPMG and PW and Lovelock and Lewes for PWC). The chartered accountants and audit firms in India are regulated by the Institute of Chartered Accountants of India (ICAI) and therefore, the Big Four must have as local members, firms registered in the name of local chartered accountants. All the audit work is handled by the local firm, which supposedly follows global standards. The global brand is still not allowed to be used in the audit business. For its part, the ICAI sees the MNCs' entry into India as a backdoor one. Thus to go and seek

HOW TO DETECT A FRAUD

ICAI has prescribed a revised standard on auditing, SA 240, that lists the responsibilities of auditors relating to fraud. The revised SA 240 will be applicable to audits on and after April 1, 2009. It says:

Rs 30 crore were reportedly found in 2002 in B. Ramalinga Raju's benami fixed deposits and accounts

DEFINITION OF FRAUD IS:

Intentional material mismanagement of the financial statements due to fraudulent financial reporting or misappropriation of assets.

AUDITORS HAVE TO

Maintain an attitude of professional scepticism, recognising the possibility of fraud, notwithstanding past experiences of a management's honesty, etc.

Identify and assess the risk of material misstatement in the financial statements due to fraud — Satyam's auditors apparently failed to do this

Obtain audit evidence by designing and implementing appropriate responses

Respond appropriately to suspected or confirmed fraud

Use discretion to determine if they can override the duty of confidentiality and blow the whistle — Seldom used

RESPONSES CAN BE

Authentication of documents by experts
Unannounced location visits/ tests
Contacting major customers/ suppliers — Satyam's auditors didn't seem to have confirmations on the margins it was earning
Interviewing personnel involved
Using computer-assisted techniques such as data-mining
Testing integrity of computer-generated records and transactions
Getting third party evidence — Satyam's auditors didn't establish third party confirmations for its debt and cash positions

FRAUDS MAY GO UNDETECTED DEPENDING ON:

Degree of collusion, skill of perpetuator, frequency and extent of manipulation, amounts involved and seniority of individuals involved

Risk of non-detection is higher for management frauds than those perpetuated by employees; management is in a unique position to perpetrate fraud because of its ability to manipulate accounting records and prepare fraudulent financial statements by overriding controls that otherwise appear fine — Satyam's case

FRAUDS HAPPEN WHEN THERE IS

Intense pressure to achieve expected (and perhaps unrealistic) earnings target or financial tcome — Satyam's case
Perceived opportunity emanating from the ability to override internal control

CHECKLIST FOR IDENTIFYING FRAUD

- ☑ Unusual or unexpected relationships
- ☑ **Suspicion or allegations of fraud**
- ☑ Unsupported or unauthorised balances or transactions
- ☑ Last-minute adjustments, significantly affecting financial results
- ☑ Evidence of employees' needless access to systems and records
- ☑ Unavailability of original documents
- ☑ Significant unexplained items on reconciliations
- ☑ Unusual changes in trends, such as receivables growing faster than revenues
- ☑ Large number of credit entries and other adjustments to receivables
- ☑ Disparities between the accounts and customers' ledgers
- ☑ Missing or non-existent cancelled checks
- ☑ Missing inventory
- ☑ Denial of access to key IT staff and those responsible for governance

WEAK LINKS IN THE AUDITING CHAIN?

BREAK-UP	JOB DESCRIPTION	% OF AUDITING WORK	WHO DOES IT
Sampling	Identifying select a/c items for verification	10	Junior Auditor (Graduates, CA articled)
Voucher Checking	Checking all expenses and sales vouchers for errors	30	—do—
Ledger Checking	Verifying voucher amounts with postings in ledgers a/c	20	—do—
Physical Verification	Physically authenticate the stock-in-trade and other assets	10	—do—
Trial Balance & Reconciliation	Tally the balances of P&L a/c and balance sheet	10	Audit Manager
Auditing	Final assessment based on the accounting standards	20	Engagement Manager & Partner

Source: *BT* Research

BIG TASK, SMALL PAY

The stipend paid to juniors appears too little.

SEMESTER	ICAI FIXED STIPEND	SALARY AT LOCAL AUDITOR	SALARY AT BIG FOUR
First Year	**1,000**	**2,500-3,000**	**5,000-6,000**
Second Year	**1,250**	**4,000-5,000**	**7,000-10,000**
Third Year	**1,500**	**6,000-7,000**	**12,000-16,000**

Stipend is in cities with population of 20 lakh & above; valid for articled CA assistants
Figures in Rs

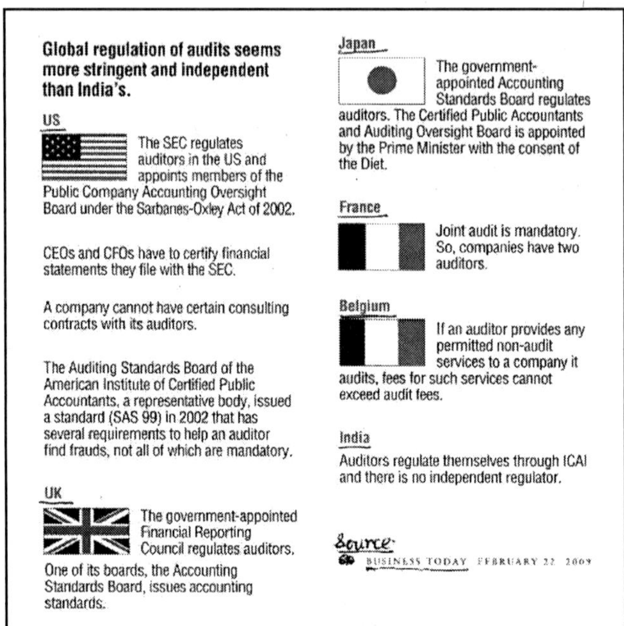

Global regulation of audits seems more stringent and independent than India's.

US

The SEC regulates auditors in the US and appoints members of the Public Company Accounting Oversight Board under the Sarbanes-Oxley Act of 2002.

CEOs and CFOs have to certify financial statements they file with the SEC.

A company cannot have certain consulting contracts with its auditors.

The Auditing Standards Board of the American Institute of Certified Public Accountants, a representative body, issued a standard (SAS 99) in 2002 that has several requirements to help an auditor find frauds, not all of which are mandatory.

UK

The government-appointed Financial Reporting Council regulates auditors. One of its boards, the Accounting Standards Board, issues accounting standards.

Japan

The government-appointed Accounting Standards Board regulates auditors. The Certified Public Accountants and Auditing Oversight Board is appointed by the Prime Minister with the consent of the Diet.

France

Joint audit is mandatory. So, companies have two auditors.

Belgium

If an auditor provides any permitted non-audit services to a company it audits, fees for such services cannot exceed audit fees.

India

Auditors regulate themselves through ICAI and there is no independent regulator.

Source: BUSINESS TODAY FEBRUARY 22 2009

auditing work as an international firm and then sign the balance sheet as an Indian firm ought not to be tolerated. But this happens in India.

The PWC's Satyam saga is now being used to re-negotiate in the WTO, a reciprocal access for Indian auditing firms to the US, the UK and to other countries in return for opening up India to the Big Four.

Foreign audit firms in India were recently allowed to advertise their services, but they're still prohibited from marketing their services. Audit in India is a smaller business for the Big Four. It however brings in anywhere between 25 and 40 per cent of their Indian revenues. Also, these firms operate through multiple entities as the Indian Partnership Act [1932] doesn't allow one body to have more than 20 partners. The new law on limited liability partnership passed in December 2008 will ease this barrier on the number of partners and clear the path for less-complicated structures.

Chapter III

The Truth about Satyam

The truth about the Satyam accounting fraud, I expect, will spill out in instalments with passage of time. Of course, besides the accounting fraud, we are now confronted with an accountability crisis as well. That is, who all are responsible and why is it taking so long to find out?

In 2001 I had returned to Harvard on my annual sojourn to teach economics for the summer term. In that capacity as an economist, I was invited to a lunch meeting with members of the Board of the New York Stock Exchange [NYSE] to speak about the Indian economic reforms. During the course of my talk, I spoke about the disclosure standards in India for business corporates. I pointed out that most Indian companies would fail to be listed in the NYSE if the US Securities and Exchange Commission's norms on disclosure were applied to them. All one has to do to find out, I said, is to see the Crisil compilation on company accounts [as illustrated in Chapter II] to infer that there is an array of corporates committing daylight accounting fraud.

As an illustration, I cited the example of one of India's multiproduct corporate giants [Reliance] that would not be able even to disclose who owned how much of its shares in their cartel of companies. I pointed to its sharp business practices used to jack up its stock price by first collecting money from the BSE by new IPOs, then lending that money at zero interest rate as inter-corporate loans to shell companies which were all completely owned by the promoter himself. In turn these shell companies went back to the BSE with the loaned funds to buy the stocks of the lending promoter's company, thereby driving up its share price, which shares in turn were mortgaged by that giant corporate for more loans! I did not sit quiet, I told the lunch gathering: I had approached the Delhi High Court which then sent my complaint to the Ministry of Company Affairs for action [which is still awaited!!]. There was considerable mirth on hearing this at the lunch. Board members asked me for a copy of my court petition which I did send to them.

Only later I understood why they were amused and so curious to know about the corporate giant: two months later, this giant corporate failed to get listed in the NYSE, and had to withdraw its application to be listed, and never since has its application to be listed ever been entertained again, while twelve other Indian companies including Satyam have got listed. At that stage I had not studied about Satyam affairs, but I learn now that in 2001 itself, the then Secretary for Economic Affairs in the Ministry of Finance, Dr. E.A.S. Sarma IAS, had apprised the Ministry of Company Affairs and the SEBI about Satyam's land fraud, and the inquiry ordered into his complaint is still in progress! The only official action taken on it however was to ease out Dr. Sarma from the Ministry. He chose to take pre-mature retirement, rather than be transferred to the Ministry of Coal.

The moral of this narration is that Satyam is not the first, nor the last gigantic rip-off of the Indian public. It represents not only the ruination of the retail share buying middle class [2.07 lakh investors holding 5.27 crores Satyam shares in just two trading sessions saw the price per share fall from Rs.179.10 to Rs.23.85] but also of the poorer classes who faithfully deposit their savings in public sector banks, which in turn lend to Satyam [the company market cap fell from Rs.15,262 crores to just Rs.1607 crores]. No doubt these banks are re-capitalised by the government but that is by a higher fiscal deficit and hence inflation. The important question is therefore why such sophisticated plunder of the nation takes place with very little punishment. *That is the accountability crisis of today.*

Part of the answer to how such frauds happen is in Ramalinga Raju's letter of January 7, 2009 to the Satyam Board of Directors [Annexure]. This letter of confession was incidentally triggered by the indictment of Satyam by the World Bank. Thereafter it would have been only a matter of time before the accounting can of worms of Satyam would spill out. So Raju decided to cut his losses and confess. On page 3 of his letter at point 2 he states that during the last two years, Rs. 1230 crores "was arranged (not reflected in the books of Satyam) to keep the operations going ... by giving all kinds of assurances." The questions that arises are: How arranged, on what assurances, and to whom? Only the Board may know at present. The accurate and true answer to these three questions will unearth what is going on not only in Satyam, but also in corporates that, with a few exceptions, are growing by leaps and bounds in apparent profits. But Satyam gets first prize for sheer audacity and brazenness.

India's biggest corporate fraud, Satyam, broke out as a confession of a Rs.7,000 crore account fabrication. The fraud has now attained the dimensions of *fraudulent diversion of funds, money laundering, foreign exchange manipulation insider trading, criminal breach of trust, income-tax violation* and round-tripping of ill-gotten wealth.

On January 7, 2009, B. Ramalinga Raju, then chairman of Satyam Computer Services Ltd revealed in a letter to the Board that he had, over the years, *fudged the company's books to the tune of at least* Rs. 7,000 crore (see Annexure). The disclosure came three

07 Jan 2009 10:53AM HP LASERJET FAX p.2

To the Board of Directors

Satyam Computer Services Ltd.

From B. Ramalinga Raju

Chairman, Satyam Computer Services Ltd. January 7, 2009

Dear Board Members,

It is with deep regret, and tremendous burden that I am carrying on my conscience, that I would like to bring the following facts to your notice:

1. The Balance Sheet carries as of September 30, 2008

   a. Inflated (non-existent) cash and bank balances of Rs.5,040 crore (as against Rs. 5361 crore reflected in the books)

   b. An accrued interest of Rs. 376 crore which is non-existent

   c. An understated liability of Rs. 1,230 crore on account of funds arranged by me

   d. An over stated debtors position of Rs. 490 crore (as against Rs. 2651 reflected in the books)

2. For the September quarter (Q2) we reported a revenue of Rs.2,700 crore and an operating margin of Rs. 649 crore (24% Of revenues) as against the actual revenues of Rs. 2,112 crore and an actual operating margin of Rs. 61 Crore (3% of revenues). This

07 Jan 2009 10:53AM HP LASERJET FAX p.3

has resulted in artificial cash and bank balances going up by Rs. 588 crore in Q2 alone.

The gap in the Balance Sheet has arisen purely on account of inflated profits over a period of last several years (limited only to Satyam standalone, books of subsidiaries reflecting true performance). What started as a marginal gap between actual operating profit and the one reflected in the books of accounts continued to grow over the years. It has attained unmanageable proportions as the size of company operations grew significantly (annualized revenue run rate of Rs. 11,276 crore in the September quarter, 2008 and official reserves of Rs. 8,392 crore). The differential in the real profits and the one reflected in the books was further accentuated by the fact that the company had to carry additional resources and assets to justify higher level of operations –thereby significantly increasing the costs.

Every attempt made to eliminate the gap failed. As the promoters held a small percentage of equity, the concern was that poor performance would result in a take-over, thereby exposing the gap. It was like riding a tiger, not knowing how to get off without being eaten.

The aborted Maytas acquisition deal was the last attempt to fill the fictitious assets with real ones. Maytas' investors were convinced that this is a good divestment opportunity and a strategic fit. Once Satyam's problem was solved, it was hoped that Maytas' payments can be delayed. But that was not to be. What followed in the last several days is common knowledge.

I would like the Board to know:

1. That neither myself, nor the Managing Director (including our spouses) sold any shares in the last eight years – excepting for a small proportion declared and sold for philanthropic purposes.

2. That in the last two years a net amount of Rs. 1,230 crore was arranged to Satyam (not reflected in the books of Satyam) to keep the operations going by resorting to pledging all the promoter shares and raising funds from known sources by giving all kinds of assurances (Statement enclosed, only to the members of the board). Significant dividend payments, acquisitions, capital expenditure to provide for growth did not help matters. Every attempt was made to keep the wheel moving and to ensure prompt payment of salaries to the associates. The last straw was the selling of most of the pledged share by the lenders on account of margin triggers.

3. That neither me, nor the Managing Director took even one rupee/dollar from the company and have not benefitted in financial terms on account of the inflated results.

4. None of the board members, past or present, had any knowledge of the situation in which the company is placed. Even business leaders and senior executives in the company, such as, Ram Mynampati, Subu D, T.R. Anand, Keshab Panda, Virender Agarwal, A.S. Murthy, Hari T, SV Krishnan, Vijay Prasad, Manish Mehta, Murali V, Sriram Papani, Kiran Kavale, Joe Lagioia, Ravindra Penumetsa, Jayaraman and Prabhakar Gupta are unaware of the real situation as against the books of accounts. None of my or Managing Director's immediate or extended family members has any idea about these issues.

Having put these facts before you, I leave it to the wisdom of the board to take the matters forward. However, I am also taking the liberty to recommend the following steps:

1. A Task Force has been formed in the last few days to address the situation arising out of the failed Maytas acquisition attempt. This consists of some of the most accomplished leaders of Satyam: Subu D, T.R. Anand, Keshab Panda and Virender Agarwal , representing business functions, and A.S. Murthy, Hari T and Murali V representing support functions. I suggest that Ram Mynampati be made the Chairman of this Task Force to immediately address some of the operational matters on hand. Ram can also act as an interim CEO reporting to the board.

2. Merrill Lynch can be entrusted with the task of quickly exploring some Merger opportunities.

3. You may have a 'restatement of accounts' prepared by the auditors in light of the facts that I have placed before you.

I have promoted and have been associated with Satyam for well over twenty years now. I have seen it grow from few people to 53,000 people, with 185 Fortune 500 companies as customers and operations in 66 countries. Satyam has established an excellent leadership and competency base at all levels. I sincerely apologize to all Satyamites and stakeholders, who have made Satyam a special organization, for the current situation. I am confident they will stand by the company in this hour of crisis.

In light of the above, I fervently appeal to the board to hold together to take some important steps. Mr. T.R. Prasad is well placed to mobilize support from the government at this crucial time. With the hope that members of the Task Force and the financial advisor, Merrill Lynch (now Bank of America) will stand by the company at this crucial hour, I am marking copies of this statement to them as well.

Under the circumstances, I am tendering my resignation as the chairman of Satyam and shall continue in this position only till such time the current board is expanded. My continuance is just to ensure enhancement of the board over the next several days or as early as possible.

I am now prepared to subject myself to the laws of the land and face consequences thereof.

(B. Ramalinga Raju)

Copies marked to:

1. Chairman SEBI
2. Stock Exchanges

weeks after Satyam's board *approved a merger of Maytas Infra Ltd and Maytas Properties Pvt. Ltd*, two companies promoted by the Raju family with the software firm. *The deal* was scrapped just a day later in the face of shareholder backlash. The worms had turned! *Satyam's shares plunged* and the *company hired DSP Merrill Lynch Ltd* to help it address the situation. While going through Satyam's books, the finance firm discovered what it terms "material irregularities," and it reported *these to regulators on 6 January*. Raju thus came clean a day later, and not before being found out.

Events moved rapidly after that. Raju and several of his associates were arrested. As were the auditors of Price Waterhouse, Satyam's then auditor. The board was dismissed by the government that put in place a new board. And later, a new chief executive, albeit an insider, was appointed.

The scam at Satyam Computer Services, began with a successful effort on the part of investors to thwart an attempt by the minority-shareholding promoters to use the firm's cash reserves to buy out two companies owned by them—Maytas Properties and Maytas Infra. That aborted attempt at expansion precipitated a collapse in the price of the company's stock and a shocking confession of financial manipulation and fraud from its Chairman, Ramalinga Raju.

What we were told was that over an extended period of time, the Raju promoters decided to inflate the review and profit figures of Satyam. That is, the company had a huge hole in its balance sheet, consisting of non-existent assets and cash reserves that have been recorded and liabilities that are unrecorded. According to the confessional statement of Raju, the balance sheet shortfall was more than Rs. 7000 crore.

The revenue of India's IT industry has grown at a compound annual rate of almost 30 per cent in the past eight years, driven by exports. This is remarkable, assuming that revenue and profit

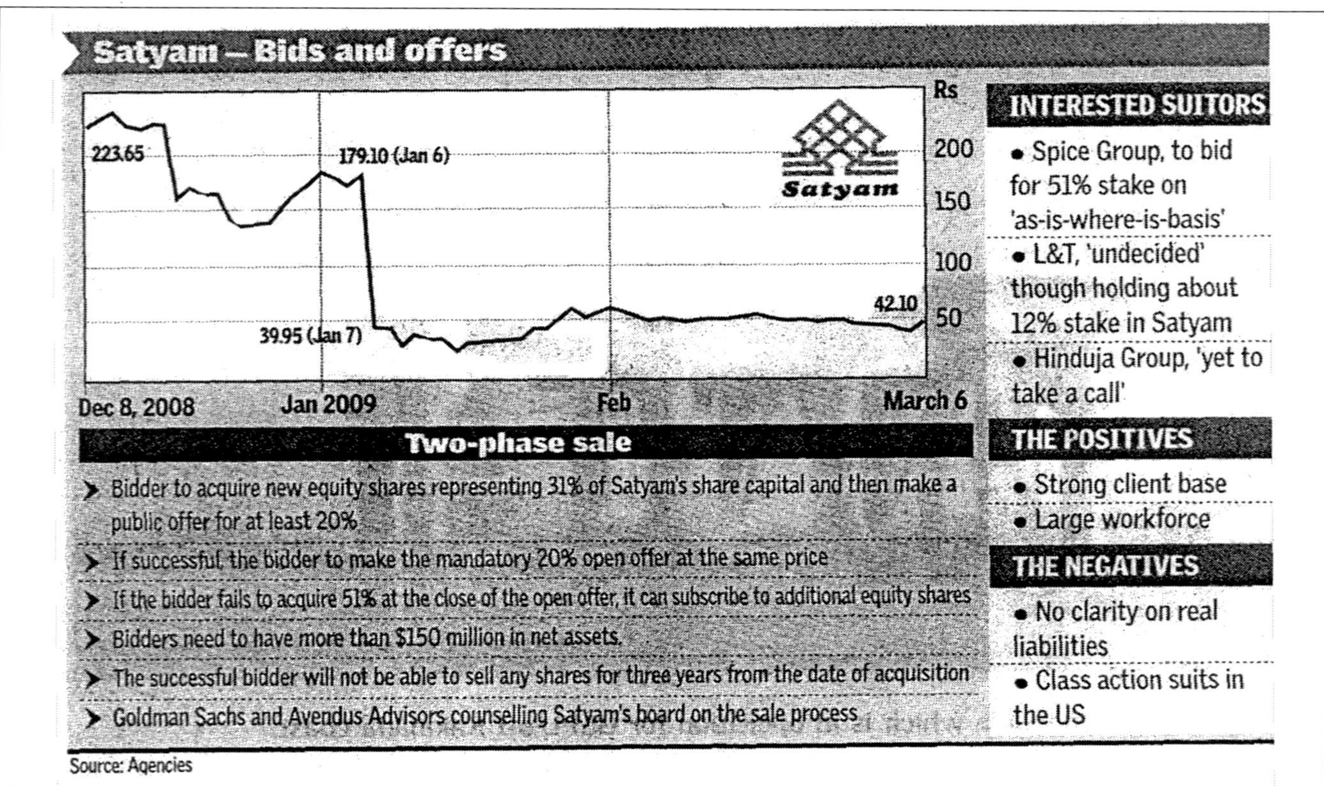
Satyam — Bids and offers
Rs
200
150
100
50
223.65
179.10 (Jan 6)
39.95 (Jan 7)
42.10
Satyam
Dec 8, 2008
Jan 2009
Feb
March 6
INTERESTED SUITORS
• Spice Group, to bid for 51% stake on 'as-is-where-is-basis'
• L&T, 'undecided' though holding about 12% stake in Satyam
• Hinduja Group, 'yet to take a call'
THE POSITIVES
• Strong client base
• Large workforce
THE NEGATIVES
• No clarity on real liabilities
• Class action suits in the US
Two-phase sale
➤ Bidder to acquire new equity shares representing 31% of Satyam's share capital and then make a public offer for at least 20%
➤ If successful, the bidder to make the mandatory 20% open offer at the same price
➤ If the bidder fails to acquire 51% at the close of the open offer, it can subscribe to additional equity shares
➤ Bidders need to have more than $150 million in net assets.
➤ The successful bidder will not be able to sell any shares for three years from the date of acquisition
➤ Goldman Sachs and Avendus Advisors counselling Satyam's board on the sale process
Source: Agencies

inflation have not excessively overstated performance. With cheap skilled labour having shored up profits that were lightly taxed when compared with the norm, net profits must have been substantial and rising too. Why then did the fourth largest IT company choose to take the criminal route of falsifying accounts and indulging in fraud? Why did a leading company in one of India's most successful industries of recent years need to inflate profits?

In the year 2000, Satyam Computer merged with a related company, Satyam Enterprises. Raju's cousin, C. Srinivasa Raju, who held 800,000 shares, or 19 per cent, in Satyam Enterprises, was reportedly allotted an equivalent number in Satyam Computer.

The stake of the promoters fell sharply after 2001 when they held 25.60 per cent of equity in the company. This fell to 22.26 per cent by the end of March, 2002, 20.74 per cent in 2003, 17.35 per cent in 2004,15.67 per cent in 2005,14.02 per cent in 2006, 8.79 in 2007, 8.65 at the end of September 2008, and 5.13 per cent in January 2009 (Business *Line,* January 3, 2009). The most recent decline is attributed to the decision of lenders from whom the family had borrowed, to sell the shares that were pledged with them. But the earlier declines must have been the result either of sale of shares by promoters or of sale of new shares to investors. According to audited balance sheet figures (if they are to be trusted) available from the CMIE's database, the paid-up equity in Satyam Computer Services rose from Rs. 56.24 crore in March 2000 to just Rs. 64.89 crore by March 2006 and further to Rs. 133.44 crore in March 2007. Overall, the number of shares held by the promoter group fell from 7.16 crore (22.8 per cent) to 5.8 crore (8.6 per cent) between September 2001 and September 2008.

Two things are clear at this point in time. First, that the Satyam scandal is much more than just what Raju confessed to as a accounting manipulation. It is a massive multi-dimensional fraud that, like an onion, appears to have several layers, and Raju is clearly not the only person involved. The scale and extent of the fraud appears to go much beyond Satyam and probably extends to the political class, whose ill gotten money has been laundered for a steady "dividend."

The second is that a massive exercise in obfuscation of the facts of the case appears to be on. Selective "facts" of the fraud are being either spelt out in Court or leaked out deliberately. The information is coming out in dribbles, building up a mystique. Importantly, it is also sending people on a diversionary path.

Thus, the latest "fact" that has been revealed is the employee count of Satyam. The police counsel told the Court that the actual employee headcount was lower by as much as 13,000 compared to the 53,000 employees that the company disclosed as late as September last. Raju is said to have siphoned off Rs. 20 crore a month from Satyam through salaries for these ghost employees.

How did Raju manage this feat? With banks strictly following KYC norms, how could he open 13,000 ghost accounts which would have required as many signatures, addresses, proof of such addresses and IT PAN numbers? Raju must be a master forger if he managed to forge the required documents. More important, he must have had an entire back-office devoted to just managing these ghost accounts!

Satyam is no "mom and pop" corner shop. It is a full-fledged corporate entity with professionals manning its HR and finance functions. Besides, it has enterprise resource planning (ERP) in place and it is not possible to perpetrate such frauds without the connivance of several people. So, are there others who were hand-in-glove with Raju in his nefarious activities? Assuming there were, it is impossible to imagine how so many people could keep such a major secret to themselves for so many years.

So the inflation of employee rolls is a red herring designed to send investigators, regulators and the media on a leather hunt. In fact, there are reasons to suspect that the "confession" itself is one big red herring designed to divert focus from the main issue of defalcation of Satyam's cash.

That there has been an illegal, unfair draining of cash from Satyam by Raju is now certain. What is not certain though is how he managed the feat, how long has he been doing it, how much he has drained out and who his accomplices are in the fraud, both within the company and outside. These questions will be followed by the big one: on where he has invested the ill-begotten wealth. Here again, there are reports of benami land deals across Andhra Pradesh but, again, these could also be red herrings.

The logical question is: why are so many diversions being created and who is doing this? Are there powerful interests that could be hurt if the real truth, *satyam,* comes out? Is Satyam an accounting, civil, criminal and securities fraud, all rolled into one. It is only the combined expertise that can get to the bottom of the matter. The importance of getting to the bottom of this dreadful act cannot be over-emphasised for the stakes have increased significantly since the fraud first came to light.

The government has to act and act quickly to uncover the fraud in all its (in)glorious detail and to send Raju and his accomplices to their logical destination: Jail. The country's image is at stake and any attempt at a cover-up can be damaging. What we need is a *real* investigation of the case; not the kind of stuff we have been seeing in the last few months.

As Charles Correa, noted architect states*: "Earlier industrialists and then defence contractors financed political parties. Now real estate does, especially in the states because chief ministers have easier access to it. The kickbacks are huge" (Interview, Times of India, 10 September 2008).*

Indeed, it was Satyam's proposed takeovers of Maytas the real estate firm that set in motion the events that have led to the near collapse of Satyam itself. Was the selected bidder for the Hyderabad Metro Rail Project (HMRP) favoured even before the final tendering was over? Does it point to a "political scam?" The managing director of Delhi Metro Rail Corporation (DMRC), E Sreedharan, made several such scathing remarks in a letter to the Deputy Chairman of the Planning Commission, Montek Singh Ahluwalia, on 11 September 2008 and even more explicitly in another article later (*Indian Express* October 31, 2008). Shaken by the exposure from its own consultant, the HMRP officials reacted strongly and also in a belittling manner, demanded an unconditional apology, and threatened to file a defamation suit. Sreedharan refused to apologise. The DMRC and the Government of Andhra Pradesh (GOAP) parted ways.

Sreedharan was reacting to a major policy shift in the Government of India (GOI) to operationalise all future urban metro projects under the build-operate-transfer (BOT) model solely under the private sector. It may be recalled that it was a consortium including two Hyderabad-based real estate companies, Navbharat and Maytas, which bagged the contract for the Rs. 12,132 crore project and offered a royalty of Rs. 30,311 crore to the GOAP. In this consortium, the dominant player is Maytas, the real estate firm owned by the sons of the Chairman of information technology major, Satyam Computers. A new company, Maytas Metro Limited (MML), was floated by the successful consortium and signed the contract with GOAP on 19 September 2008.

Maytas had no previous experience of building and operating a metro rail. It got eligibility for bidding because of its tie-up with Ital-Thai, which was involved in the construction of the Bangkok skytrain. After bagging the contract to construct and run the HMRP this new company was named MML. The share of Ital-Thai seems to be only 5% in MML. The originally intended share of Ital-Thai in this consortium is not known. In tune with the present GOAP'S controversial (and scandalous) policy of allocating large tracts of land to corporate companies, Maytas has been trying to get 2,500 acres at Machchilipatnam port. Riding on the positive image of the information technology sector and (before the scandalous revelations in January 2009) of Satyam Computers, in a short time, Maytas had emerged as an important real estate company with ventures in hundreds of acres (special economic zones) on the outskirts of Hyderabad.

Maytas is now believed to be looking at expanding the metro rail project not just to make its bid viable but also to get more value for its properties by providing connectivity. The government seems to have agreed to give the company the opportunity to expand routes and therefore additional land.

The feeling that this selection of the bidder looks like a "settlement" in the context of land allocations, real estate and politics in Andhra Pradesh (as in Charles Correa's observation), and of the future plans of Maytas gains strength in view of the objections raised by Sreedharan and the presence of several pro-Maytas clauses in the concession agreement.

The promotional hoardings of Maytas on Hyderabad's streets for its real estate venture, Maytas Hill County, proclaim: "Soon, there will be nothing left." One hopes this does not become true for democracy, its institutions and the politics.

The Satyam fraud has shaken the country's audit profession and regulatory authorities to its roots. Has there been a systemic failure or is Satyam just an exception? Has the macro structure of the audit procedure evolved in a manner commensurate with the growth of Indian business and its physical globalisation?

Thereafter the Securities and Exchange Board of India (SEBI) and the Department of Corporate Affairs (DCA) made it mandatory to have audit committees where independent directors were in a majority and whose chairman had to be an independent director; they would be (a) obliged to review and implement internal controls; (b) observe accounting standards; (c) review and approve accounts; (d) review financial management and; (e) appoint internal auditors and recommend statutory auditors. Their recommendations are binding on the Board unless the Board discloses to the shareholders its reasons for non-agreement. My own experience in three cases is that a strong knowledgeable audit committee and its chairman are the best bulwark whenever promoters' opinion differs from that of the auditors. We should substantially strengthen this system.

The Institute of Chartered Accountants of India (ICAI) [and also, the Institute of Company Secretaries of India (ICSI)] have been strongly supportive of moves for quality improvement and quality controls. ICAI issued 32 Accounting Standards, 34 Auditing Standards, 6 Internal Audit Standards and several External Quality Control Standards. It has moved for harmonisation of standards with the International Federation of Accountants (IFAC). ICAI also brought in monetary limitations on the non-audit work that auditors can provide to the auditee company directly or through related parties. Where the partners of the audit firm or their relatives have a 20 per cent beneficial interest, the fee from all such assignments cannot exceed the audit fee.

Yet, Satyam happened. While Satyam's external auditors are in the limelight, the responsibility also rests with the Chief Executive Officer (CEO), the Chief Financial Officer (CFO), internal auditors and the audit committee. Their roles should be examined by a joint special study group of the MCA and ICAI so that remedial steps can be taken. The Vivian Bose Commission in India and the Sarbanes Oxley Act in the US have strengthened the system of audit and corporate regulation in the public interest.

For the audit profession, Satyam is indeed a blot. The Satyam incident will level the field for auditors, and there in now concern for the role of audit and the devolving of responsibility for financial fraud in company accounts.

Raju and his son, had also picked up substantial land in and around Hyderabad. Maytas Infra, the company that out bid Anil Ambani's company, Essar, to win the Hyderabad metro contract, was hoping to use the growing appreciation of its land bank to pay-off the Andhra Pradesh (AP) government in the next 30 years. The other two bidders were asking for government investment to build this project. *Delhi Metro Chief E Sreedharan had called the grant of the project to Maytas a scam.*

At that time the AP government had threatened him with a defamation suit. Maytas sources claim that Sreedharan was a consultant to the project and it was surprising that he chose to object to it. They allege that the bidders that had lost out in the race were trying to bag the metro project due to the controversy. They also referred to the manner in which Anil Ambani's company had been awarded the ultra mega power plant after Lanco—another Hyderabad-based company—the original winner of the bid, was found to be inadequate. What is really worth watching is whether the Satyam chief and his patrons in the AP government and the Centre manage to hang on to the Hyderabad metro project.

The state CID claims that Raju siphoned off Rs 7,000 crores from his accounts. He resorted to printing counterfeit fixed deposits of various banks and rigging muster rolls—less people were employed then stated: just 40,000 compared to 53,000. This helped him to siphon out their salaries through bogus accounts. He resorted to routing his dubious funds through Mauritius, into his real estate. He would have got away with this fraud if the valuation of the real estate had not come down due to economic slowdown.

If he had pulled off the take-over by Satyam of Maytas Infra and Properties then there would have been no scandal.

Price Waterhouse Coopers (PWC), their auditors, never blew the whistle on Raju's shenanigans. Quite obviously, they were in cahoots. Otherwise what was the reason that DSP Merrill Lynch discovered Raju's fraud in three days and PWC could not do it in seven years. Merrill Lynch, which was going through the books before it chose to take over the company, reportedly discovered a discrepancy in the output per employee—which seemed fake. Closer enquiry revealed that Satyam was a house of cards with many jokers.

Now there is a clear attempt to enable Satyam to survive. Why? Ideally, the company should have been allowed to go bust, but the government, extraordinarily, appointed directors on its board, many of whom have a conflict of interest.

Without doubt, the Raju brothers have perpetrated what the 14th Additional Chief Metropolitan Magistrate, Hyderabad, N. Victor Immanuel described as "the rarest of rare cases of fraud, which merited categorising as exceptional." Immanuel is also the presiding officer of the designated court for CBI cases.

About the Satyam Fraud, till today, the single-most crucial question, "Where did all that money go," remains unanswered.

The answer is not easily available even though CBI officials have seized and sealed computers and servers hoarding millions of bytes of information. After the arrest of Ramalinga Raju, the only thing that CBI investigations have unravelled is that the maze is far deeper than they originally thought. The mandatory 90-day period to file the preliminary chargesheet is unlikely to reveal much of what happened. Though the Raju brothers were arrested on January 10 and Vadlamani a couple of days later, investigations into the allegations and charges have not kept pace for the authorities to list them vividly in a chargesheet by April 9.

Sleuths of the Central Bureau of Investigation (CBI) probing the Rs. 7,136-crore Satyam Fraud had hit a technical hurdle. Wading through millions of bytes stored in hard disks of computers is hard enough. But the officers discovered that the conspirators of the con had deployed biometric entry barriers at different levels to prevent entry into databases.

There are multiple agencies involved—the Criminal Investigation Department (CID) of the Andhra Pradesh Police, Securities and Exchange Board of India (SEBI), Serious Fraud Investigation Office, (SFIO) Enforcement Directorate, (ED), Income Tax (I-T) authorities and CBI—and that the investigations had to be started afresh after CBI took over from the CID on February 18 on a state government request. This has caused some confusion in the investigation. The investigators may have found many valuable leads in the accounting fraud and financial malfeasance; but there is not enough to give a clear picture of who scammed who and how, and where the loot has disappeared.

Now there is a totally fresh case of the CBI under a new First Information Report (FIR); and therefore, the specially constituted Multi-Disciplinary Investigation Team (MDIT) of the CBI keeps approaching a specially designated court to ask for more time to frame supplementary charge-sheets after extensive investigations, seeking refuge under the special law governing its functioning. The delays have added fuel to theories of a political conspiracy to hush it up.

However a wealth of data has enabled the CBI to put together some 53,000 documents gathered from searches so far, besides an array of computers and servers that may yield forensic evidence on what exactly was done to siphon off money and stash it away through the 357 companies floated by the Raju brothers and others in the Satyam promoter group.

However, the CBI has gathered enough evidence to prove how Satyam Computers' revenues were inflated and it is probing rotation of funds and the role of front companies. They have found that the accused generated fake invoices, showing imaginary money being pumped into the financial system and profits which were never there. There are also strong leads on insider trading; and therefore, the CBI is trying to understand the share transactions of the Satyam group companies on the National Stock Exchange (NSE) and the Bombay Stock Exchange (BSE). The funds realised by offloading shares were used to buy 1,500 properties.

The 16-member MDIT led by V.V. Lakshmi Narayana, an IPS officer of the rank of deputy inspector-general of police operating from a fortified office in Hyderabad, with finance, banking, accounts and auditing experts, faces a gigantic task as none of the five in custody—the Raju brothers, Vadlamani and two ex-auditors S.Gopalakrishnan and Srinivas Talluri—are forthcoming. The case against them is of criminal conspiracy, criminal breach of trust, cheating, forgery, using forged documents and falsification of accounts. But a breakthrough is yet to come.

In the early phases of questioning, the accused kept saying that they were not aware of how the fraud had been executed. However, the huge pile of documents seized, coupled with electronic evidence relating to fudging of records through fake bank accounts, fictitious invoices and balance sheets is expected to help investigators establish the nature of and, at least, some aspects of the fraud. They are also seeking details of the land deals from the state Revenue Department.

Some leads gathered so far point to Satyam producing fake invoices to show that it had got Rs 5,000 crore from sales in New York. MDIT is now probing whether the money was rerouted when Satyam bought some nine companies in the US and other countries at a higher price and the extra sums were rerouted into India. With the SFIO, SEBI, ED and I-T Department teams sharing expertise and information, the MDIT may be able to

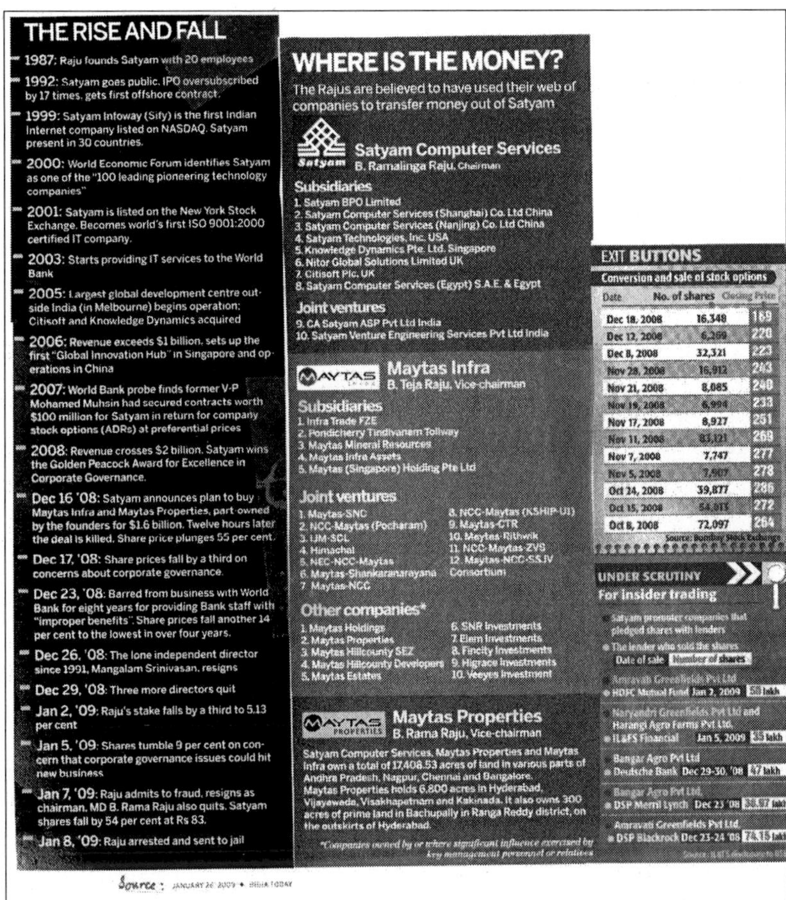

THE RISE AND FALL

- **1987:** Raju founds Satyam with 20 employees
- **1992:** Satyam goes public. IPO oversubscribed by 17 times, gets first offshore contract.
- **1999:** Satyam Infoway (Sify) is the first Indian Internet company listed on NASDAQ. Satyam present in 30 countries.
- **2000:** World Economic Forum identifies Satyam as one of the "100 leading pioneering technology companies"
- **2001:** Satyam is listed on the New York Stock Exchange. Becomes world's first ISO 9001:2000 certified IT company.
- **2003:** Starts providing IT services to the World Bank
- **2005:** Largest global development centre outside India (in Melbourne) begins operation; Citisoft and Knowledge Dynamics acquired
- **2006:** Revenue exceeds $1 billion, sets up the first "Global Innovation Hub" in Singapore and operations in China
- **2007:** World Bank probe finds former V-P Mohamed Muhsin had secured contracts worth $100 million for Satyam in return for company stock options (ADRs) at preferential prices
- **2008:** Revenue crosses $2 billion. Satyam wins the Golden Peacock Award for Excellence in Corporate Governance.
- **Dec 16 '08:** Satyam announces plan to buy Maytas Infra and Maytas Properties, part-owned by the founders for $1.6 billion. Twelve hours later the deal is killed. Share price plunges 55 per cent.
- **Dec 17, '08:** Share prices fall by a third on concerns about corporate governance.
- **Dec 23, '08:** Barred from business with World Bank for eight years for providing Bank staff with "improper benefits". Share prices fall another 14 per cent to the lowest in over four years.
- **Dec 26, '08:** The lone independent director since 1991, Mangalam Srinivasan, resigns
- **Dec 29, '08:** Three more directors quit
- **Jan 2, '09:** Raju's stake falls by a third to 5.13 per cent
- **Jan 5, '09:** Shares tumble 9 per cent on concern that corporate governance issues could hit new business
- **Jan 7, '09:** Raju admits to fraud, resigns as chairman. MD B. Rama Raju also quits. Satyam shares fall by 54 per cent at Rs 83.
- **Jan 8, '09:** Raju arrested and sent to jail

WHERE IS THE MONEY?

The Rajus are believed to have used their web of companies to transfer money out of Satyam

Satyam Computer Services
B. Ramalinga Raju, Chairman

Subsidiaries
1. Satyam BPO Limited
2. Satyam Computer Services (Shanghai) Co. Ltd China
3. Satyam Computer Services (Nanjing) Co. Ltd China
4. Satyam Technologies, Inc. USA
5. Knowledge Dynamics Pte. Ltd. Singapore
6. Nitor Global Solutions Limited UK
7. Citisoft Plc. UK
8. Satyam Computer Services (Egypt) S.A.E. & Egypt

Joint ventures

9. CA Satyam ASP Pvt Ltd India
10. Satyam Venture Engineering Services Pvt Ltd India

Maytas Infra
B. Teja Raju, Vice-chairman

Subsidiaries
1. Infra Trade FZE
2. Pondicherry Tindivanam Tollway
3. Maytas Mineral Resources
4. Maytas Infra Assets
5. Maytas (Singapore) Holding Pte Ltd

Joint ventures
1. Maytas-SNC
2. NCC-Maytas (Pocharam)
3. IJM-SCL
4. Himachal
5. NEC-NCC-Maytas
6. Maytas-Shankaranarayana
7. Maytas-NCC
8. NCC-Maytas (KSHIP-U1)
9. Maytas-CTR
10. Maytas-Rithwik
11. NCC-Maytas-ZVS
12. Maytas-NCC-SSJV Consortium

Other companies*
1. Maytas Holdings
2. Maytas Properties
3. Maytas Hillcounty SEZ
4. Maytas Hillcounty Developers
5. Maytas Estates
6. SNR Investments
7. Elem Investments
8. Fincity Investments
9. Higrace Investments
10. Veeyes Investment

Maytas Properties
B. Rama Raju, Vice-chairman

Satyam Computer Services, Maytas Properties and Maytas Infra own a total of 17,408.53 acres of land in various parts of Andhra Pradesh, Nagpur, Chennai and Bangalore. Maytas Properties holds 6,800 acres in Hyderabad, Vijayawada, Visakhapatnam and Kakinada. It also owns 300 acres of prime land in Bachupally in Ranga Reddy district, on the outskirts of Hyderabad.

*Companies owned by or where significant influence exercised by key management personnel or relatives

EXIT BUTTONS

Conversion and sale of stock options

Date	No. of shares	Closing Price
Dec 18, 2008	16,348	169
Dec 12, 2008	6,269	220
Dec 8, 2008	32,321	223
Nov 28, 2008	16,912	243
Nov 21, 2008	8,085	240
Nov 19, 2008	6,994	233
Nov 17, 2008	8,927	251
Nov 11, 2008	83,121	268
Nov 7, 2008	7,747	277
Nov 5, 2008	7,907	278
Oct 24, 2008	39,877	286
Oct 15, 2008	[illegible]	272
Oct 8, 2008	72,097	264

Source: Bombay Stock Exchange

UNDER SCRUTINY
For insider trading

- Satyam promoter companies that pledged shares with lenders
- The lender who sold the shares

Date of sale | Number of shares

- Amravati Greenfields Pvt Ltd
  - HDFC Mutual Fund Jan 2, 2009 [illegible] lakh
- Naryandri Greenfields Pvt Ltd and Harangi Agro Farms Pvt Ltd.
  - IL&FS Financial Jan 5, 2009 [illegible] lakh
- Bangar Agro Pvt Ltd
  - Deutsche Bank Dec 29-30, '08 47 lakh
- Bangar Agro Pvt Ltd.
  - DSP Merrill Lynch Dec 23 '08 [illegible] lakh
- Amravati Greenfields Pvt Ltd.
  - DSP Blackrock Dec 23-24 '08 [illegible] lakh

Source: JANUARY 26 2009 ♦ INDIA TODAY

unravel most of what transpired at Satyam during the Raju regime and where the missing cash, whatever its exact value, has been spirited away and whether it can be traced to the last paisa. The SFIO has found that the company had about 70 bank accounts in other countries. It is to question the accused separately and verify whether Raju alone, or with his brother, handled select bank accounts with large sums as deposits as well as correspondence for the placing, renewing or confirmation of deposits.

SEBI has estimated a loss of over Rs 20,000 crore for investors in the Satyam scrip worldwide after the January 7 sensational statement about fraud by Raju. Its investigations have shown that auditors Gopalakrishnan and Talluri played a lead role in creation of artificial demand for the Satyam scrip by certifying overstated financial results of the company as true. "The market value erosion suffered by investors in January alone was Rs 13,500 crore. The auditors did not raise a single objection to irregularities in financial statements in 32 audit meetings since their appointment as statutory auditors of the company," said CBI's Public Prosecutor T. Venkataramana. Significantly, the auditors were found to have frequently changed their passwords while working on computers and the irony is investigators have to spend time in numerous decoding exercises.

There is also considerable legal damage. The first comes from the UK based mobile solutions company: *Upaid System* that has filed in a Texas court a lawsuit for fraud and forgery against Satyam. Therein, it has claimed damages of $1 billion. The suit is to come up for hearing against Satyam in Texas on June 1, 2009. Upaid is however willing for an out-of-court settlement. Then there are 13 class action lawsuits, filed following Raju's sensational statement, which implies that the company may have to pay out hundreds of millions of dollars if the US courts decide that the burden of the scandal falls on the company, its promotors and auditors. The next four months are perhaps crucial for Satyam. As investigators try and put the pieces of the jigsaw together to draw a picture, Satyamites will hope the Government will not wait for the political carnival called "elections" and move on with the auction process instead of despatching them to the recycle bin, or selling it off to some MNC. I would suggest that Government take it over, and then in instalments sell the equity to the public till it become a public limited company. No Government should try to protect the Satyam fraudsters, nor should the public tolerate it. Instead the Government has found it convenient to sell the Satyam to Tech Mahindra, which is represented on the Board of the Satyam!

Moreover, on April 6, 2009, the Central Bureau of Investigation (CBI) charged Satyam Computers former chairman B Ramalinga Raju with fudging balance sheets, creating forged bank deposits and fake invoices for years in an attempt to keep the share price of the company at a higher level.

CBI has charged that he had fudged accounts with eight others accused in India's biggest-ever corporate fraud. The agency has also submitted 1,532 documents—including statements of 433 witnesses—to Nampally Metropolitan Court in Hyderabad. The chargesheet papers, packed in 25 trunks, were brought to the court in a mini van. While the chargesheet itself is 300 pages long, the annexures run into a mammoth 65,000 pages.

There are nine accused in the case: Raju and his two brothers Rama Raju and Suryanarayana Raju, former CFO Vadlamani Srinivas, Price Waterhouse (PW) auditors S. Gopalakrishnan and Talluri Srinivas, Satyam Vice-President G. Ramakrishna, Senior Finance Manager D. Venkatapathi Raju, and Assistant Finance Manager C. Srisailam. They have been accused and charged with criminal conspiracy, cheating, impersonation, forgery of valuable security, forgery for the purpose of cheating, showing forged documents as genuine, falsification of accounts and causing disappearance of evidence, under eight sections of IPC. If proven the charge under Section 467 alone could lead to a sentence of life imprisonment.

The 80-page chargesheet filed in a city court said financial irregularities were done in active connivance with the company's statutory auditors from 2001 to 2008.

The chargesheet however has left out D. Gopalakrishnam Raju, general manager of SRSR Services, who had also been arrested by the state CID in connection with the Satyam case. It is to be seen if he turns approver at a later stage. The case will now go to trial but many questions remain unanswered.

There are nine accused in the case: While the CBI investigations have provided some answers, there are still questions that need satisfactory replies. For example the chargesheet did not touch on the diversion of funds by the Raju brothers or anyone else. According to CBI DIG V. V. Lakshmi Narayana, "We will file a supplementary chargesheet if further investigations reveal something." The CBI also claims that while it is probing the cash trail, it has proof that Raju forged fixed deposit receipts to show balances that were non-existent. Raju also used 327-odd fron companies to secure loans for the promoter family.

Question	What the CBI has to say
Why did Raju confess when he did?	He was close to being caught and wanted to save himself the embarrassment of being forced into a corner. The CBI also feels Raju has only let on a part of what he knows.
Was it a Rs. 7,000-cr or a Rs. 10,000 cr fraud?	The chargesheet puts the figure at about Rs. 7,800 crore but it could be closer to Rs. 10,000 crore.
How long has this been going on?	Since 2001
Who all were involved?	Chargesheet names Ramalinga Raju, Rama Raju, Suryanarayana Raju, V. Srinivas, S. Gopalakrishnan, T. Srinivas, G. Ramakrishna, D. Venkatapathi Raju, and C. Srisailam.
Was the money ever there?	No details in chargesheet, but CBI has proof that Raju forged fixed deposit receipts to show balances that were non-existent. SFIO and I-T department are also investigating.
What will be Raju's fate?	If proven, the charge under section 467 alone would impose a life imprisonment on the accused while the punishment for remaining charges may vary from 2 to 7 years in jail.
Did Price Waterhouse (PW) know?	ICAI had said that Satyam's former CFO told them neither partner of PW was involved. But CBI DIG Narayana says,

	"The clean chit from ICAI will not affect investigations."
Will the truth ever be known?	While many questions have not been sufficiently answered, CBI claims when it has more evidence, it will file a supplementary chargesheet. But not very conclusive.
Who will take over Satyam?	Not for chargesheet to answer. Process taking place simultaneously. Revelations could have a bearing on potential suitors.

Source: Business World, April 13, 2009.

Though there were indications in the past that Raju might have diverted the company's funds for other purposes, which was even hinted at by Union Corporate Affairs Minister P. C. Gupta, the chargesheet did not make any mention of it. It more or less endorsed what Ramalinga Raju had 'confessed' in his infamous e-mail of January 9. However, CBI sources said they would focus on diversion of funds from now on since the primary task of filing the chargesheet in time had been met.

According to the chargesheet, the accused intentionally committed the financial fraud only to keep the share price up and this had misled investors into believing that the company was doing well. Over a period of time, when the share price was at a high level, Raju and his family members off-loaded their holding and thereby, made huge profits and raked in Rs. 700 crores. This was, in turn, pumped into fictitious companies that they had floated in the names of their family members and trusted employees. The ill-gotten money was then invested in the real estate through 'benami' companies.

As per the chargesheet, the agency has found the origins of fraud and its modus operandi to be as follows: "The accused, through their balance sheets, gave an impression that they were doing extremely well, when they were not. This helped in roping in more foreign investment and more business partners." The chargesheet also notes that the accused showed high profits to dupe Indian shareholders, who rushed to buy company shares at inflated prices. The chargesheet also says that Raju and other operators periodically offloaded their promoter shares and forged their bank accounts' papers and statements. And thus earned a windfall Rs. 700 crores for the family.

But earlier, during interrogation, Satyam's Srinivas had told members of the Institute of Chartered Accountants of India (ICAI) that teh company's sales were inflated and bank statements had been forged to justify the claim. He said the firm has 600 odd major clients, some of whose sales receipts were doubled. As per Srinivas's confession to ICAI, the whole scam started as an adjustment of Rs. 10 crore around five to six years, ago, and the malpractice continued quarter after quarter before it attained unmanageable proportions in the second quarter of 2008.

Earlier this week, ICAI had confirmed that Srinivas had made it clear to them that neither partner of PW was involved. But Narayan says, "The clean chit from ICAI will not affect investigations. We will depend on our investigation to prove the guild."

As stated by Ramalinga Raju in his confessional e-mail of January 9, the balance sheet for teh second quarter of 2008 had shown non-existent bank balances to the tune of Rs. 5,103 crore, while in reality the bank balance was only Rs. 61 crore. Similarly, the accrued interest shown in the balance sheet was Rs. 376 crore while the actual interest paid by the banks was only Rs. 7.42 lakh.

From April 2003 to December 2008, about 74,625 fake invoices were generated in the Invoice Management System (IMS). Along with teh invoices, the accused also inflated sales. As against the actual sale of Rs. 23,434 crore from the first quarter of 2004 to the second quarter of 2008, the sales figure was jacked up to Rs. 27,691 crore.

In the bargain, investors, both the general public and public sector banks, lost heavily. For instance, the Life Insurance Corporation of India (LIC) itself lost a staggering Rs. 950 crore, while UCO Bank , Punjab National Bank, Union Bank of India, Corporation Bank, Indian Bank, Allahabad Bank and the Oriental Bank of Commerce have lost Rs. 10 crore.

In 1992, the Rajus, the original promoters, held 18.78 percent shares. On May 31, 1995, five companies were floated by Ramalinga Raju and other members of the family. In 2000-2001, through these companies, the promoters sold Rs. 75 crore worth shares and the money was gifted to Ramalinga Raju.

The total amount received by the promoters through off-loading the shares was Rs. 707 crore and their holding in the company dropped to 8.59 per cent in 2006.

Of the nine accused, eight are in judicial custody and are lodged inside the Chanchalguda jail in Hyderabad. The ninth, Raju's younger brother B. Suryanarayana Raju—a director of SRSR Advisory Services, a financial services advisory to the family's firms—has not been directly implicated. He has been named only in the cases pertaining to diversion of funds to Maytas for acquiring land and in the case of benami companies to secure loans for the promoter family. Suryanarayana had obtained bail from a local court on 5 March. CBI officials believe that Suryanarayana, who was the intermediary for several land deals, may be able to provide them clues about the missing money in the next phase of investigation.

But despite the CBI's extensive documentation, it has not been able to come up with satisfactory answers to the what query as to what the Raju brothers and their partners did with the money. Other investigating agencies such as the Serious Frauds

Investigation Office (SFIO) and the Income Tax (I-T) Department are also assessing the amount siphoned from Satyam, based on the seized records. CBI has also been unable to answer the question about the inflation in the number of employees in Satyam's offshore operations.

It is also believed that the CBI will send Letters Rogatory to the US Justice Department seeking details of Raju's accounts in Bank of Baroda's New York branch. Raju and his family are believed to have accounts in banks in the US and that could be the focus of the supplementary chargesheet expected to be filed later this week.

Many claim that this hurried filing of the chargesheet was an attempt to oppose the Rajus' bail application. But while the first step has been taken to hasten the process, there are still many glaring loopholes that need to be plugged before the truth becomes known.

Chapter IV

THE SPECTRUM FRAUD

The operations and functions of the Indian telecom industry were monopolised by department of telecom (DOT) until 1994. The DOT set-up in 1984, acted as the policymaker, regulator and operator for all those services that existed in the industry then. The allocation of spectrum for different purposes was and is managed by the Wireless Planning and Coordination (WPC) of the Ministry of Communications. Eventually, after almost 10 years since the establishment of the DOT, there arose a realisation that telecom services on demand at affordable and reasonable prices combined with a world class standard for their quality of services must be provided as charted out in the National Telecom Policy 1994 (NTP-'94). NTP 94 recognised that the required resources for achieving these targets must also come through private investments and the involvement of the private sector is mandatory to bridge the resource gap.

In the year of 1995, there began auctioning of the spectral band for global systems for mobile (GSM) cellular operations alone. As the first step towards auctioning of the GSM spectral band of 20 services, India was divided into 21 circles—six states forming six "A" circles, eight states forming eight "B" circles and 12 states forming seven "C" circles. The four metros—Delhi, Mumbai, Chennai and Kolkata—were considered as separate areas of operations. This stage of auctioning of 20 spectram was called "direct auctioning" and was conducted in two stages. Two qualified bidders who quoted the highest prices for the circle emerged as the winners in the second stage. This stage of auctioning had a few shortcomings: first, though there was considerable privatisation of the telecom industry, the service roll-out still remained slow. This was apparently due to the fact that the winners had shelled out huge sums to win a circle and hence, had financial crunches to provide faster services. Second, various non-winners of the bidding process had complained of a lack of transparency in the auctioning process, while the winners complained of high inter-circle interconnection costs fixed by the DOT. These were believed to be the reasons for the slow service roll-outs.

In order to resolve the above issues and to create a regulatory structure, the Telecom Regulatory Authority of India (TRAI) was set-up in 1997 and the New Telecom Policy '99 (NTP99) was announced. The focus of the NTP99 was telecommunication for all and telecommunication within the reach of all. It offered a new scheme to the bidders called the "migration package," according to which the existing service operators could make a one-time payment called "entry fee" and subsequently pay, on a quarterly basis, a licence fee, which is a part of their adjusted gross revenue (AGR).

Spectral auction is one of the major sources of revenue available to a government. With a booming telecom sector and its net worth of approximately $ 30 billion, the contribution of communication sector to Indian GDP has increased from about 1.59 per cent in 2000 to 3.97 per cent in 2006. It becomes imperative for India to choose a proper auction design to maximise government revenue comparable to other countries like the US, UK, Germany, Switzerland, etc. At the same time, emphasis must be given to safeguard the interests of telecom operators and ensure the future growth of the telecom sector and not just keep in mind the profits from auctions.

Worldwide, the third generation licences were awarded either through "a beauty contest" or other auctioning methods such as sealed bidding, open bidding, simultaneous multiple round auctions and Vickrey auction. The beauty contest is an auctioning procedure, which is not wholly dependent on the pricing. With much similarities to an actual "beauty contest," here too, every contestant will have to convince the auctioneers of their ability to provide services. Based on answers to questions like—how wide the service area will be, how swiftly and efficiently services will be rolled out and what will be the customer usage charges—a contestant will be selected as the winner of this "beauty contest" and will be provided the licence.

Some of the methods followed by various countries and their profitability rating is shown in the Table below:

The advantage of a "beauty contest," when compared to open auctions, is that the operators will be able to work on 3G side-by-side, even as they keep on focusing on the provision of mobile services to those who are still unconnected and who remain a priority.

Table: Spectral Auctioning Design (Various Countries)

Country	Method of Licence Distribution	Key Aspects	Year	S&P* Profitability Rating
Finland	Beauty contest	First country to award 3G licences. It was not price based. Four operations	1999	Average
Japan	Beauty contest	Three operators	2000	Excellent
France	Beauty contest + auction	$4.5 billion per licence for the two licences and later auctioning for remaining two licences	2001	Very good
UK	Auction	Five licences—four for established Operators and only one for a new operator	2000	Very good
US	Simultaneous multiple round auction	Reserve price set to $10 billion	2004	Good

*Standard and Poor's (S&P) is a division of McGraw-Hill that publishes financial research and analysis.

Source: Sivasankar, S.V et al "Spectrum Auctioning and Licensing."

The Spectrum fraud, the greatest fraud since 1947, represents a swindle of about Rs. 50,000 crores of public money. The Union Telecommunication Minister A. Raja is charged with having allotted 2G spectrum for mobile services on a "first-cum-first served basis" rather than going for an open global auction. He is also charged with having allotted spectrum in excess of the stipulated 6.2 megahertz. The Delhi High Court has admitted a Public Interest Litigation against the Spectrum allocation. The Central Vigilance Commission has questioned his ambiguous and political-patronage-driven move. Raja defends himself with the claim that he had not deviated from the allocation practice followed by his predecessor. Note that his predecessor also belonged to the same political party (DMK) and functioned according to the dictates of his party Supremo Karunanidhi till he was sent out of the Ministry. Recently he (predecessor) has atoned for his "sins" and has been rehabilitated and his is no more persona non grata there. Telecom's Spectrum is the only hotly demanded item that has not registered an increase in the last 7 full years, of the price fixed in 2001 i.e., from the time the rate was fixed in 2001, till the allocation was made in 2008.

The contrived Swan Telecom and Unitech which got most of the Spectrum are two companies which have no experience what so ever in Telecommunication. Other companies involved are interlinked with two companies e.g., Tiger, Parrot and Zehra—all zoological names. Little is known as to who are the people behind these mysterious companies.

Unitech, a real estate company, got a huge share of the Spectrum without investing anything in telecom infrastructure. It got licences to operate in 22 circles for Rs. 1651 crores. Within weeks, it sold 60% shares for 6120 crores to the Norwegian company Telenor, currently a major telecom player in Pakistan and Bangladesh. The Home Ministry has yet to clear the Telenor deal, as it is operating in Pakistan and Bangladesh.

Annexure -1: Swan Telecom Private Limited

A. Swan Telecom Private Limited (the "Company") was incorporated on 13th July 2006 as Swan Capital Private Limited with registered office at 7th Floor, Raheja Point- 1, Jawaharlal Nehru Marg, Vakola Market, Santa Cruz (E), Mumbai – 400 055. The subscribers to the Memorandum of Association were:

Person	No. of equity shares of Rs. 10 each
Himanshu Agarwal (employee of ADA Group)	1
Powersurfer Interactive (India P Ltd. (A ADA Group Co.	4,999
Reliance Energy Management Services P Ltd. (an ADA Group Company)	5,000
Total	10,000

On 22nd January 2007, the Company allotted equity shares of Rs. 10 each as given below:

Person	No. of equity shares of Rs. 10 each
Tiger Trustees Pvt Ltd (*formerly Tiger Traders Pvt Ltd*)	27,03,000
Reliance Telecom Limited (a wholly owned subsidiary of Reliance Communications Limited)	2,97,000
Total	30,00,000

On 2nd March 2007, the Company further allotted equity shares of Rs. 10 each as given below:

Person	No. of equity shares of Rs. 10 each
Tiger Trustees Pvt Ltd (formerly Tiger Traders Pvt Ltd)	9.55,06,000
Reliance Telecom Limited (a wholly owned subsidiary of Reliance Communications Limited)	1,04.94,000
Total	10,60,00,000

The Company made an application for Unified Access Service Licence (UASL) on 2nd March 2007 and the shareholders of the Company on that date were:

Shareholder	No. of shares	Percent
Tiger Trustees Pvt Ltd (formerly Tiger Traders Pvt Ltd)	9,82.19,000	90.10%
Reliance Telecom Limited (a wholly owned subsidiary of Reliance Communications Limited)	1,07.91,000	9.90%
Total	10,90,10,000	100.00%

B. Tiger Trustees Private Limited was incorporated on 20th March 2006 as Tiger Traders Private Limited with registered office at Reliance Energy Centre, 3rd Floor, Santacruz East, Mumbai-400 055. The shareholders of Tiger Trustees Private Limited as on 2nd March 2007 were;

Shareholder	No. of shares	Percent
Swan Infonet Services Private Limited (formerly) Parrot Consultants Private Limited	5,000	50.00%
Swan Advisory Services Private Limited (formerly Zebra Consultants Private Limited)	5,000	50.00%
Total	10,000	100.00%

The directors of Tiger Trustees Private Limited on incorporation were:

Name of the Director	No. of shares
Mr. Ashish Karyekar (employee of ADA Group)	704, Reliance Energy Quarters, Chembur, Receiving Station, Deonar, Mumbai-400 088.
Mr. Paresh Rathod (employee of ADA Group)	204, Reliance Energy Quarters, Chembur, Receiving Station, Deonar, Mumbai-400 088

C. Swan Infonet Services Private Limited was incorporated on 17th March 2006 as Parrot Consultant Private Limited with registered office at Reliance Energy Centre, 3rd Floor, Santacruz East, Mumbai-400 055. The shareholders of Swan Infonet Services Private Limited as on 2nd March 2007 were:

Shareholder	No. of shares	Percent
Tiger Trustees Private Limited (formerly Tiger Traders Private Limited)	5,000	50.00%
Swan Advisory Services Private Limited (formerly Zebra Consultants Private Limited)	5,000	50.00%
Total	10,000	100.00%

The directors of Swan Infonet Services Pvt. Ltd. on incorporation were:

Name of the Director	No. of shares
Mr. Ashish Karyekar (employee of ADA Group)	704, Reliance Energy Quarters, Chembur, Receiving Station, Deonar, Mumbai-400 088.
Mr. Paresh Rathod (employee of ADA Group)	204, Reliance Energy Quarters, Chembur, Receiving Station, Deonar, Mumbai-400 088

D. Swan Advisory Services Private Limited was incorporated on 21st March 2006 as Zebra Consultants Private Limited with registered office at Reliance Energy Centre, 3rd Floor, Santacruz East, Mumbai-400 055. The shareholders of Swan Infonet Services Private Limited as on 2nd March 2007 were:

Shareholder	No. of shares	Percent
Tiger Trustees Private Limited (formerly Tiger Traders Private Limited)	5,000	50.00%
Swan Infonet Services Private Limited (formerly Parrot Consultants Private Limited)	5,000	50.00%
Total	10,000	100.00%

The directors of Swan Infonet Services Pvt. Ltd. on incorporation were:

Name of the Director	No. of shares
Mr. Ashish Karyekar (employee of ADA Group)	704, Reliance Energy Quarters, Chembur, Receiving Station, Deonar, Mumbai-400 088.
Mr. Paresh Rathod (employee of ADA Group)	204, Reliance Energy Quarters, Chembur, Receiving Station, Deonar, Mumbai-400 088.

VALUATION PUZZLE

The government lost thousands of crores while issuing licences to new telecom companies

List of new licensees

Company	What they paid (Rs cr)	No. of circles	What they might have paid (Rs crore)	Loss to govt (Rs crore/licence)
Datacom Solutions	1,651	22	10,000	8,349
Swan Telecom	1,051	14	3,122	2,071
Loop Telecom	1,576	21	4,000	2,424
Stel	1,651	22	4,000	2,349
Shyam Telelink	1,651	22	10,000	8,349
Unitech Wireless	1,651	22	11,620	9,969

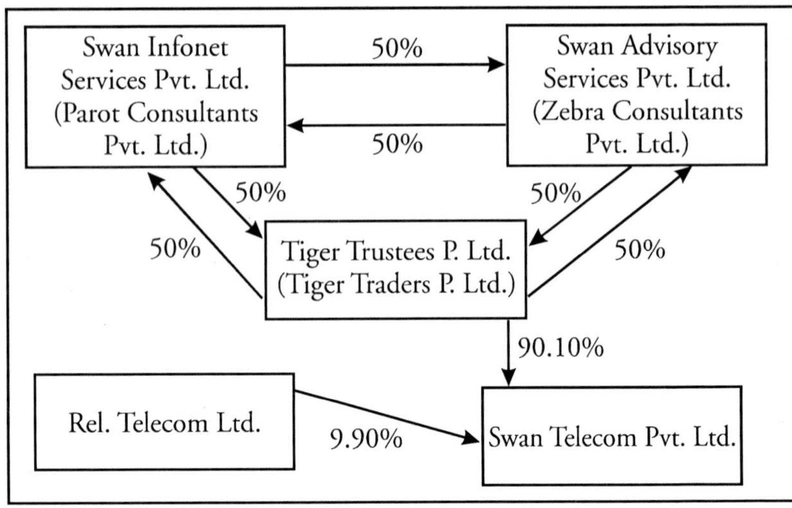

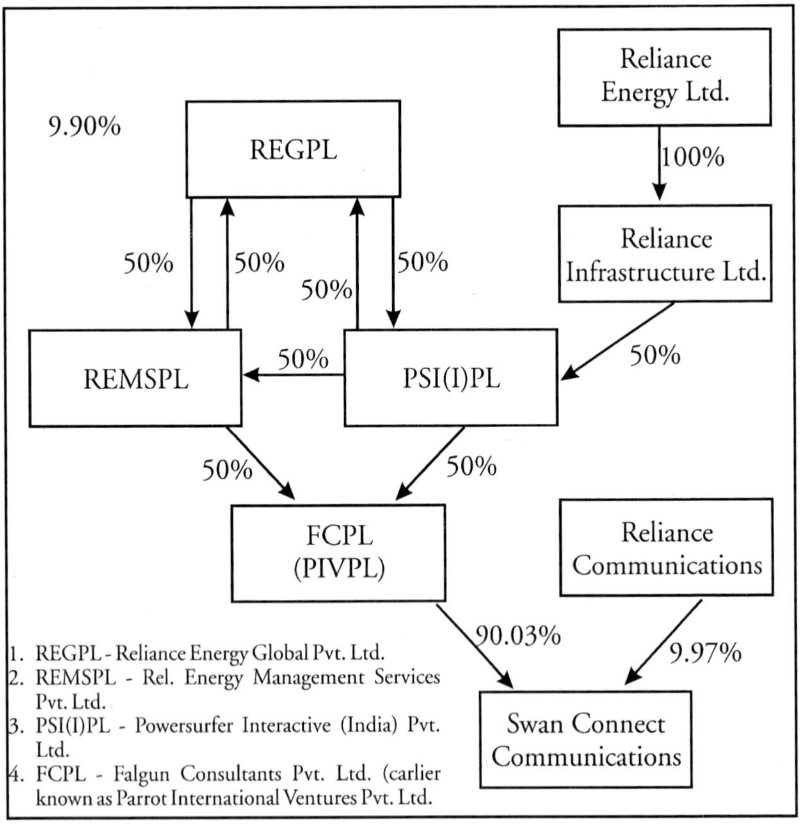

Reliance Energy Ltd.

9.90%

REGPL

100%

50%

50%

50%

50%

Reliance Infrastructure Ltd.

REMSPL

50%

PSI(I)PL

50%

50%

50%

FCPL (PIVPL)

Reliance Communications

90.03%

9.97%

Swan Connect Communications

1. REGPL - Reliance Energy Global Pvt. Ltd.
2. REMSPL - Rel. Energy Management Services Pvt. Ltd.
3. PSI(I)PL - Powersurfer Interactive (India) Pvt. Ltd.
4. FCPL - Falgun Consultants Pvt. Ltd. (earlier known as Parrot International Ventures Pvt. Ltd.

The Swan Telecom bagged the licence for Rs. 1537 crores for operating in 13 circles. Within weeks it sold 45% of shares to Etisalat, the telecom giant in UAE for 900 million US dollar (Rs.4500 crores).

Swan Telecom is now in the process of investing Rs.1000 crores by taking 49 % share in a company operating in Chennai called Green House promoters Pvt. Limited. In the Board of Directors in this Green House is Minister Raja's wife M. A. Parameswari! Raja's official address 2A, Motilal Nehru Marg is provided as the business address in Form 32 document of Registrar of Companies in Chennai!! The Minister did not inform the Prime Minister on his wife's business, (which is mandatory as per Conduct of Business Rules for Ministers), because of clash of interests: since September 2004 the Minister's wife is also a Director on the Board of another Chennai based Real Estate company-Equaas estate. The first year Balance Sheet shows this company had Rs. 755 crores as domestic turnover.

More alarming, Green House is also operating in Singapore as Greenhouse Promoters (S) Pvt Limited from Serangoon Plaza, 320, Serangoon Road, Singapore. The Minister's his relatives company Greenhouse thus has violated the Foreign Exchange Regulation by opening its Singapore office, without informing Finance and RBI authorities.

The Minister of Communications Shri A. Raja in a reply to a question in Parliament (Lok Sabha Starred Question # 232, 15.12.2008) has claimed that neither the Central Vigilance Commission (CVC) nor the Telecom Regulatory Authority of India (TRAI) has raised any objection to the allocation of Spectrum to 2G Telecom Service Providers on a 'first come first served' basis. This is nothing but an attempt to mislead the Parliament, to obfuscate matters and to conceal the truth: In a letter dated 15.11.2008, the CVC had expressed dissatisfaction

ORMATION TECHNOLOGY

THE HINDU • BUSINESS LINE
SATURDAY, NOVEMBER 22, 2008

'Spectrum allotted in line with TRAI norms'

Ministry gives point-by-point reply to CVC query

Press Trust of India
New Delhi, Nov. 21

Spectrum to new players was given on fixed licence fees, and not auctioned, according to the recommendations of the Telecom Regulatory Authority of India, the Communication Ministry, target of criticism on the subject, said on Friday.

Responding to queries from the Central Vigilance Commission amid allegations from political parties that Rs 50,000 crore was lost to the Government in distribution of spectrum, the Telecom Ministry said it had gone by the book and had done nothing wrong.

Mr A. Raja

"In the context of the auction of 2G spectrum, TRAI had observed that any differential treatment to a new entrant vis-a-vis the incumbent will go against the principle of level playing field," DoT said in its reply to the Central Vigilance Commission.

When contacted, senior DoT officials said in the 2G (existing mobile services), band allocation through auction may not be possible as the service providers were allocated spectrum at different times of their licences and the amount of spectrum with them varied in quantity.

"Therefore, TRAI felt that to decide the cut-off after which the spectrum should be auctioned will be difficult and it might raise the issue of level playing field," DoT said in a five-page point-by-point reply to the CVC.

NOT SALE

Replying to another query with regard to the sale of stakes by two new operators – Swan and Unitech – allegedly at huge premium, DoT said "the promoters of these companies have not sold their share holding but made strategic partnership for investment in the company". The licensor said these companies had stated that the investments brought in by their foreign partners would be used for rolling out services and this could enhance their capital base keeping the absolute shareholding of the promoters in tact. "Thus the question of their making windfall profits does not arise," DoT said.

DoT officials said the Finance Ministry is of the view that foreign investment through dilution of equity of new telecom companies brings in FDI for roll-out of the services. At the same time, promoters' equity should not be allowed for sale, said the official.

To further press the case, the issue of prohibition of sale of promoters' equity for Unified Access Services licence holders is under the deliberation of the DoT.

3G AUCTION

Responding to the query of the commission on the process of 3G spectrum auction process, DoT said existing operators as well as new players would be eligible to participate in the auction and the reserve price has been fixed at two times of what was recommended by TRAI.

'TRAI to decide on number of players'

Press Trust of India
New Delhi, Nov. 21

The Government on Friday ruled out limiting the number of operators in a circle and said that any such decision would need to be reverted back to telecom regulator TRAI.

The Department of Telecommunications has so far considered applications for telecom licences that were received till September 25, 2007, and is yet to take a decision on those that came between September 25 and October 1.

This had led to widespread speculation that the applications after September 26 would not be taken up at all and there would be a cap in that sense.

Speculation got reinforced because of the scarcity of spectrum and there being about 12 players in circles (once new telcos start operations), which offers sufficient competition.

"We have not taken such a decision ... I don't think the Telecom Commission has taken such a decision (either). If at all, it again has to be referred to TRAI. I never asked the Commission to deliberate on the issue," the Telecom Minister, Mr A. Raja, said.

APPLICANTS

DoT had received 575 applications, of which 343 were filed between September 26 and the cut-off date of October 1, 2007.

There were 24 applicants in this period including AT&T, DLF, Moser Baer, Ispat, and Sterlite. A total of 46 companies had applied for telecom licences. Licences are given on a first-come-first-served basis.

A senior DoT official said the move would invite litigation from the affected companies and the Government would honour all applications but gradually. They will not be taken up in a hurried manner.

The DoT in a press release on January 10, 2008, had said: "TRAI on August 28, 2007, recommended that no cap be placed on the number of access providers in any service area. The Government has accepted this recommendation of TRAI Trai ... "Accordingly, the DoT has decided to issue letter of intent to all eligible applicants who applied (on and before) September 25, 2007."

Annexure 2

8 EMERGING BUSINESS & IT THE ECONOMIC TIMES ON SATURDAY NEW DELHI 29 NOVEMBER 2008

Trai rebuts Raja claim, says DoT ignored call for 2G auctioning

Our Bureau
NEW DELHI

TRAI chairman Nripendra Misra has refuted telecom minister A Raja's claim that department of telecom (DoT) went ahead with the first-come-first-serve (FCFS) basis to allot 2G licences to new players on the basis of Trai recommendations. Mr Misra said Trai had recommended auctioning of 2G licences but the telecom department chose to ignore its suggestion.

The Trai chairman said market forces should have determined the price of a licence, which includes start-up spectrum. "We had recommended a mechanism for giving licences which must capture the market price. DoT had not sought our views on whether spectrum was to be auctioned or not," he said.

"We had recommended a mechanism for giving licences which must capture the market price. DoT had not sought our views on whether spectrum was to be auctioned or not"

NRIPENDRA MISRA
CHAIRMAN, TRAI

The DoT had earlier stated in reply to the central vigilance commission (CVC) that it had gone by the guidelines laid by Trai. Telecom minister A Raja has been repeatedly accused of favouring a few players to grant the 2G licences and for selectively quoting Trai recommendations to go ahead with the FCFS formula.

But Mr Misra said DoT had bypassed Trai's initial recommendation and did not adopt the auction route. He was speaking at the round-table conference on 'India Telecom Landscape 2012', organised by industry body CII.

Mr Misra also said that the process of spectrum management must capture the three cardinal features of good governance—predictability, stability and transparency. "The entire decision-making mechanism in the telecom sector should be in the public domain," said Mr Misra.

He said Indian telecom sector has remained unaffected in the adverse global trend. "The current global financial crisis is now one of the major constraints on the pace of economic reform, but the Indian telecom sector is one of the few sectors that have remained almost unaffected," said Mr Misra.

over an earlier response of the Department of Telecom (DoT) to the Commission's queries on the policy for the allocation of spectrum (See Annexure A). The CVC had asked for specific clarifications on various issues related to spectrum allocation, including licensees like Swan selling their equity at high values to Etisalat without making any progress in operationalising mobile telephony, terming this as a "highly unethical practise." As far as the TRAI is concerned, its Recommendations of October 2003 clearly state that new licenses have to be allocated through a multi-stage auction process. The DoT has violated this recommendation while allocating new licenses to 2G Telecom Service Providers on a 'first come first served' basis. The TRAI had in fact repeatedly warned the DoT (both before the Letters of Intent (LoIs) were issued, as well as after 120 LoIs were issued on 10.01.2008 but before licenses were signed) about the legal provisions relating to implementing TRAI recommendations.

In a letter to the DoT on 14.01.2008, the TRAI Chairman pointed out that its recommendations cannot be implemented either in bits and pieces or while ignoring interlinkages between various recommendations. In the "Recommendations on Review of license terms and conditions and capping of number of access providers" made on 28.08.2007, the TRAI had stated:

"The allocation of spectrum is after the payment of entry fee and grant of license. The entry fee as it exists today is, in fact, a result of the price discovered through a markets based mechanism applicable for the grant of license to the 4th cellular operator. In today's dynamism and unprecedented growth of telecom sector, the entry fee determined then is also not the realistic price for obtaining a license. Perhaps, it needs to be reassessed through a market mechanism."

The Minister of Communications wilfully disregarded the TRAI recommendation and allocated new licenses in an arbitrary manner, which has resulted in an enormous loss to the national exchequer.

Sitaram Yechury, the leader of the CPI (M) group in Rajya Sabha, had written to the Prime Minister in 29.2.2008 to forewarn the Government on the impropriety of issuing new licenses under 2G spectrum at throwaway prices on a "first come first served" basis. It was mentioned in that letter that the market price of the spectrum, which was being allocated along with these licenses, was 6 to 7 times higher than the price paid by these new licensees. The 2001 price paid was clearly outdated since it was the outcome of a multi-stage auction held 7 years back, when there were only 4 million subscribers in India as against 300 million subscribers now.

CPI (M)'s warnings have now been confirmed with the two deals struck by two of the licensees. Swan Telecom (September

2008) and Unitech (October 2008), with two foreign telecom companies, Etisalat and Telenor respectively, at prices that were 5.7 and 7 times more than what they had paid for their licenses. Thus, instead of allocating the new licenses on the basis of a public auction, the DoT manipulated norms to allocate licenses to favoured private players and to facilitate the private auction of spectrum at a later date.

The DoT had adopted an extremely sinister method in eliminating competition while granting licenses to the favoured few. The cut-off date for receiving applications, which was announced on 24.09.07 to be 1st October 2007, was arbitrarily changed to 25th September 2007 on 10.01.08 (Annex D). It is obvious that this was done in order to exclude a large number of applicants and effectively capping the number of applicants to the favoured few. All this was done violating the TRAI recommendation that no cap be placed on the number of service providers in any service area. After issuing licenses in such a sinister manner, the DoT went ahead to announce its Merger guidelines on 22.04.2008 (Annex E). Strangely, while a three year lock-in period from the effective date of the licenses was laid down in case of "Mergers," "Acquisitions" were deliberately left outside the purview of these guidelines. This paved the way for licensees like Swan and Unitech to sell their stakes at a huge premium in September/October 2008, which reflected the actual market value. The estimated loss to the national exchequer, on account of undervaluation of new licenses, amount to nearly Rs. 60,000 crore (See Table in Appendix). If one adds to this the loss to the exchequer on account of undervaluation of crossover licenses for existing CDMA operators and not charging market value of surplus spectrum from existing GSM operators, each of which amounts to Rs. 20,000 crore approximately, the telecom scam presided over by the Minister of Communications would worth nearly one lakh crore! Gross Wrongdoings.

The CPI (M) is in possession of an internal note of the DoT on the processing of pending application for licenses under 2G spectrum, signed by the then Secretary, Telecom D.S. Mathur and Member, Finance Smt. Manju Madhavan (Annex F). It clearly appears from the document that the alternative of auctioning of new licenses, in keeping with the TRAI recommendation, was very much on the Minister's table. The DoT note states:

"Existing criteria of entry fee was based on the entry fee paid by the fourth cellular operator, which was decided based on 3 stage informed ascending financial bidding at that time (year 2001). The Indian telecom sector has witnessed tremendous growth due to the continued liberalisation and has emerged as the fastest growing telecom network in the world. Therefore, the bidding/auction process will establish the entry fee based on current market perception."

Why did not the Minister of Communications opt for the auction route, despite this proposal being on his table, and instead went about allocating licenses on an arbitrary "first come first served" basis? Not only does the underlying impropriety and wrongdoings involved become clear from this, but the responsibility also falls squarely on the Minister himself.

The CPI (M) is also in possession of a letter written on 22.11.2007 by the then Finance Secretary, GOI, Shri D. Subbarao (currently RBI Governor) to the Secretary, Telecom, questioning how the crossover license fee of Rs. 1600 crore for CDMA operators was arrived at in 2007 "without any indexation, let alone current valuation," when that rate was "determined as far back as in 2001" (Annex G). This clearly shows that the Finance Ministry was fully in the know of the impropriety involved in the case.

While the Minister of Communications continues to mislead the Parliament and the larger public by obfuscating matters, what is more disturbing is the deafening silence on the part of the Prime

Minister on this issue. That there has been an enormous loss to the national exchequer due to the arbitrary allocation of 2G licenses is incontrovertible. Responsibility for the huge loss to the national exchequer must be fixed and concrete steps undertaken to recover the amount from the beneficiaries of the scam. In the light of the material being made public, demand for immediate action on the part of the Prime Minister in this regard is growing. Failure to initiate probe into the matter and fix responsibility, undertake steps to retrieve the lost revenues and review the entire gamut of spectrum allocation policies would make the entire Cabinet complicit with this gigantic scam.

Further incriminating evidence against Union Minister for Communication and Information Technology Andimuthu Raja has become available now. This indicates that Raja went against the recommendations of senior officials in the Ministry that he heads by ignoring these recommendations [not by overruling them on the file] and opting for a contentious first-come-first served (FCFS) method for allotting spectrum for use by mobile telecommunications companies.

The Minister did it by creating conditions for the topmost official, the Secretary in the Department of Telecom (DoT), D. S. Mathur, to resign, and another senior technocrat Ms. Manju Madhavan, to go in for premature retirement. Both of them had argued against the Minister's move to allot spectrum on a FCFS basis [see p.3 of the enclosed file noting]. He then inducted a bureaucrat of his choice and thus went ahread (as if the file Note did not exist), with his controversial policy of allotting spectrum with licences to a clutch of private companies at prices that were around seven times lower than prevailing market rates.

Till October 1, 2007, the DoT had received 575 applications from 46 companies for allocating of licences with spectrum. On October 18 that year, at a meeting the DoT top brass headed by the then Secretary, Telecom, D.S. Mathur, with Raja, it was pointed out that since it would not be possible to allot spectrum to all the applicants, criteria for selection of applicants should be worked out based on availability of spectrum. In a note dated October 25 [enclosed], the then Member, Finance, of the Telecom Commission, Manju Madhavan, worked out three alternatives, the first of which was the FCFS method. Madhavan, in her note, suggested two other alternatives that involved public auction of spectrum to be conducted in a transparent manner, and recommended auction.

Moreover, she stated that "due to (the) highly competitive scenario, there is a need to review the entry fee and eligibility criteria." This was precisely what Raja did not want, or rather refused to consider without recording his view on file.

What the Minister did instead is now clear. Nine companies were arbitrarily selected for allocation of spectrum on a FCFS basis, while more than three dozen other firms were kept waiting in the queue. A cut-off date for receipt of applications was announced and then changed without explanation.

Faced with a barrage of allegations, Raja has sought to justify his position by citing the National Telecom Policy of 1999, a 2003 Cabinet decision of the NDA government and a single paragraph out of a 178-page document put out by the Telecom Regulatory Authority of India (TRAI). What he has not stated is that each of these documents had finally recommended public auctions or competitive bidding as the process for discovering the true market value of the licences with spectrum that were awarded by the DoT.

Minister Raja took over from Dayanidhi Maran, as Union Minister for Environment and Forests on May 16, 2007. As Environment Minister he had come into contact with various real estate companies that had sought environmental clearances from the Ministry. Many of these real estate companies later applied for

Department of Telecommunications

Processing of pending UASL applications - subsequent to acceptance of TRAI's recommendations on " Review of license terms & conditions and capping of number of access providers"

......

Till the cut off date i.e. 1.10.2007, DOT has received 575 applications for grant of UAS licences from 46 companies for all the 22 service areas. Spectrum being scarce resource it will not be possible to allocate the spectrum in respect of all the pending UASL applications. The matter was discussed with Hon'ble MOC&IT on 18.10.2007, where Secretary (T), Member(S), Member(T), AS(T), LA(T), JS(T) and DDG(AS) were present.

It is felt that to begin with, the Licensing Branch (AS Cell) of DOT shall ascertain the availability of spectrum from WPC Wing in each service area for new GSM and CDMA operators after taking care of the needs of existing operators for expansion of network based on justification and availability. Based on availability of spectrum, selection criterion for grant of licences/ allocation of spectrum has to be followed.

Following alternatives are available.

Alternative 1:

DOT may continue to process the pending applications on first-come-first served basis in chronological order of receipt of applications in each service area as per existing procedure. LOI may be issued in seriatim to eligible companies who fulfill the eligibility conditions of the UASL guidelines available on DOT website. The time limit for acceptance of offer should be 7 days as per the existing provision of LOI and 15 days for submission of PBG, FBG, entry fee etc. No relaxation of this time limit will be given and the LOI shall stand terminated after the stipulated time period However, the applicant may have the right to apply for new UASL license again as and when the window for submission of application of new UAS License is opened again.

Alternative2:

The criteria followed for award of new licenses for UASL has to be transparent and must withstand any legal scrutiny at a later date. Due to highly competitive scenario, there is a need to review the entry fee and eligibility criteria.

In this alternative the process of bidding /auction may be adopted The following points justify this alternative:

(a) Existing criteria of entry fee was based on the entry fee paid by the fourth cellular operator, which was decided based on 3 stage informed ascending financial bidding at that time (year 2001). The Indian telecom sector has witnessed tremendous growth due to the continued libralisation and has emerged as the fasted growing telecom network in the world. Therefore, the bidding/ auction process will establish the entry fee based on current market perception.

(b) The best option seems to invite 3 stage informed ascending financial bids for deciding the entry fee for award of new licenses based on availability of spectrum to induct the stipulated number of GSM and CDMA players in each service area. Alternatively, this could be online auction.

(c) The reserve price for entry fee may be equal to the presently stipulated entry fee in the UASL guidelines are as decided. This will not only fetch more revenue to the Government but also will be a very transparent process.

(d) Applicant company may participate for bidding. New companies may also be invited to participate in the bidding upto a cut-off date, subject to fulfillment of prescribed eligibility conditions.

The bidding could be for either of two cases:

(i) for UAS licence in either of the technology (GSM or CDMA)

or

(ii) for grant of UAS licence for GSM & CDMA both. In such case they shall participate by putting two separate request in the bidding process for entry fee.

(e) Existing licensee if desires to have cross spectrum in other technology may also be included in the bidding process based on their application.

(f) In case the existing licensee if do not participate in the bidding process for cross holding of spectrum, they shall not be considered later on.

(g) Number of slots for initial spectrum shall be fixed and priority shall be assigned to the highest bidder followed by other bidders in descending order.

(h) It may be noted that this is not auction of spectrum but only permitting entry of new operators for grant of UAS licenses alongwith assured allotment of initial spectrum subject to availability.'

(i) The period for roll-out shall be counted from the date of allocation of spectrum as recommended by TRAI.

(j) There should be a cut off date for receipt of UASL applications including application for other technology (cross holding) by existing licensees.

for grant of UAS licences may be opened from time to time
d to availability of spectrum.
ocess would amount to 'No Capping' however 'First come
rve' criteria would be replaced by entry by bidding with
d initial spectrum availability.

s:

may be issued to all the applicants, after clearly stipulating that
ill be allocated based on an auction process. New applications
e invited. Based on auctions, spectrum may be allocated to these
ees. Unsuccessful applicants who deposit the entry fee and who
auction process to get spectrum, their entry fee may be refunded
token interest amount.

Manju Madhavan
M(F).

Secy (T).

MOC + IT

25.7.0

Note: Some official notings have been cut out to protect my sources.

telecom licences—such firms include Unitech, Loop (part of the Ruia group), Datacomm (Videocon) and Swan (once partly owned by the Anil Dhirubhai Ambani group)—and some of them were indeed awarded licences.

On September 25, 2007, a few hours after Unitech put in 22 applications under eight companies, the DoT issued a press release stating that it would not accept applications beyond October 1, 2007. Despite the short notice, in this period of three working days only, as many as 373 additional applications were received.

Pressure was then mounted on former DoT Secretary Mathur to sign letters of intent in favour of certain applicants but he refused to oblige. Mathur was due to retire in two months but his service was not extended. He then left. Ms. Madhavan, the then Member, Finance took premature retirement from service. On the last day of 2007, December 31, Mathur thus retired and he was replaced by Siddharth Behura (who had earlier served as Secretary, Environment and Forests, under Raja).

Exactly 10 days later, on January 10, 2008, nine licences were awarded by the DoT on a FCFS basis, causing a loss of Rs. 50,000 crores or more.

Prime Minister Manmohan Singh has yet not given this author the requisite sanction under the Prevention of Corruption Act (1988) to prosecute A. Raja on charges that have already been investigated by the Central Vigilance Commission and the Comptroller and Auditor General of India and upheld as prime facie valid.

The CVC vide letter dated November 15, 2008 has issued a Show Cause Notice to Telecom Minister A Raja who allotted new licences in 2G mobile services on a "first come, first served" basis to two novice telecom companies, Swan and Unitech. *His move is a complete violation of Clause 8 of the Guidelines for United Access Services Licence issued by the Ministry of Communication and Information Technology Development of Telecommunication. Government of India* {No.10-21/2005-BS.I (Vol.II)/49 dated December 14, 2005}. Raja is Minister of this Ministry.

Summary of Illegalities committed by A. Raja

1. The Minister gave away 2G spectrum licences on "first-come, first-served" basis in January, 2008 at the arbitrarily fixed price of Rs. 1651 crores that he claimed had prevailed at the Spectrum auction of June 2001. At that time, the number of mobile subscribers was just 4 million. In January 2008 it was 350 million, and was growing at 10 million new subscribers per month. So auction the today would have fetched Rs. 11,000 crores from each of the six Telecom vendors.

Dr. Subramanian Swamy Ph.D. (Harvard)
President, Janata Party
Minister for Commerce, Law & Justice (1990-91)
Chairman (with Cabinet rank), Commission on Labour Standards and International Trade (1994-96)
Member of Parliament (1974-99)
Professor of Economics, Indian Institute of Technology, Delhi (1969-91)
Faculty, Harvard University (1963-69, 1985-86, 2001-08 Summer)

JANATA PARTY
A-77, Nizamuddin (East) New Delhi - 110 013, India
Phone : +91 24353805 Fax : +91 24357388
Mobile : +91 9810194279 ; +91 9940203333
Website : www.janataparty.org; www.indiaright.org
E-mail : swamy@post.harvard.edu
swamy39@gmail.com

November 29, 2008.

Prime Minister,
Government of India,
New Delhi.

Sub: Permission of Sanction u/s 13, Prevention of Corruption Act {1988}.

Sir,

The Chief Vigilance Commissioner vide letter dated November 15, 2008 had issued a Show Cause Notice to Telecom Minister A. Raja, who had allotted new licences in 2G mobile services on a 'first come, first served' basis to two novice telecom companies, Swan and Unitech. His move is a complete violation of Clause 8 of the Guidelines for United Access Services Licence issued by the Ministry of Communication and Information Technology Development of Telecommunication, Government of India {No.10-21/2005-BS.I(Vol.II)/49, dated December 14, 2005}, thus causing a loss of over Rs.50,000 crores to the Government, and consequently according pecuniary benefit to others illegally.

Clause 8 has been violated as follows: While Anil Dhirubhai Ambani Group (ADAG), the promoters of Reliance Communications (R Com), had more than 10 per cent stake in Swan Telecom, the figures were manipulated and showed as 9,99 per cent holding to beat the said Clause. The documents available disclose that on March2, 2007, when Swan Telecom applied for United Access Services Licences, it was owned 100 per cent by Reliance Communications and its associates viz. Reliance Telecom, and by Tiger Trustees Limited, Swan Infonet Services Private Limited, and Swan Advisory Services Private Limited (see Annexure 1). At one or the other point of time, employees of ADAG (Himanshu Agarwal, Ashish Karyekar, Paresh Rathod) or its associate companies have been acquiring the shares of Swan

Telecom itself. But still the ADAG manipulated the holdings in Swan to reduce it to only 9.99 per cent. Ambani has now quietly sold his shares in Swan to Delphi Investments, a Mauritius based company owned by Ahmed O. Alfi, specializing in automobile spare parts. In turn, Swan has sold 45% of its shares to UAE's Emirates Telecom Corporation (Eti Salat) for Rs.9000 crores! All this is highly suspicious and not normal business transactions. Swan company got 60% of the 22 Telecom licenced areas at a throw away price of Rs.1650 crores, when it was worth Rs.60,000 crores total.

Rcom has operations in the same circles where the application for Swan Telecom was filed. Therefore under Clause 8 of the Guidelines, Swan should not have been allotted spectrum by the Telecommunication Ministry. But the company did get it on Minister's direction, which is an undue favour from him (Raja. There was obviously a quid pro quo which only a CBI enquiry can reveal, after an FIR is registered. There is no need for a P/E, because the CVC has already done the preliminary enquiry.

It has to be investigated whether two officers of the Department of Telecom – RJS Kushwaha and D. Jha, who were opposed to showing undue favour to Swan Telecom – were transferred just prior to the allotment of the spectrum.

BSNL, which has never done any roaming agreement with any operator, was forced to do a roaming agreement with Swan Telecom, ironically BSNL does not extend this facility to any other operator. It is quite clear from the agreement that those who are at the helm of affairs of BSNL worked in favour of Swan Telecom. Quite surprisingly, the 2G spectrum licences were priced at 2001 levels to benefit these private players. That was when there were only 4 million cellphone subscribers; now it is 350 million. Hence 2001 price is not applicable today.

Immediately after acquiring 2G spectrum licences both Swan and Unitech sold their stakes to foreign companies at a huge profits.

While Swan Telecom sold its stakes to UAE telecom operator Etisalat, Unitech signed a deal with Telenor of Norway for selling its share at huge premiums.

In the process of this 2G spectrum allocation, the government received only one-sixth of what it would have got had it gone through a fresh auction route. The total loss to the exchequer of giving away 2G GSM spectrum in this way – including to the CDMA operators – is over Rs.50,000 crores and is said to be one of the biggest financial scams of all times in the country.

While approving the 2G licences, Minister Raja turned a blind eye to the fact that these two companies do not have any infrastructure to launch their services. Falsely claiming that the Telecom Regulatory Authority of India had approved the first-cum-first served rule, Raja went ahead with the 2G spectrum allocation to two debutants in the Telecom sector. In fact earlier TRAI had discussed the spectrum allocation issue with existing services providers and suggested to the Telecom Ministry that spectrum allocation be made through a transparent tender and auction process. This is confirmed by what the TRAI Chairman N. Misra told the CII organized conference on November 28, 2008 {Annexure 2}. But Raja did not bother to listen to the TRAI either and pursued the process on 'first come, first served' basis, benefiting those who had inside information, causing a loss of Rs.50,000 crores to the Government. His dubious move has been to ensure benefit to others at the cost of the national exchequer.

According to an uncontradicted report in CNN-IBN news channel of November 26, 2008, you are said to be "very upset with A. Raja over the spectrum allocation issue". This confirms that an investigation is necessary, for which I may be given Sanction so that the process of law can be initiated.

I therefore write to demand the grant of Sanction to prosecute Mr. A. Raja, Minister for Telecom of the Union of India for offences under the Prevention of Corruption Act. The charges in brief are annexed herewith {Annexure 3}.

Warm Regards

Yours sincerely,

(SUBRAMANIAN SWAMY)

Encls: a/a

Hence the loss by freezing the price at the June 2001 level arbitrarily, is about Rs. 50,000 crores net.

2. The "First-come, first-served" basis was rejected as arbitrary and biased by the Delhi High Court in a PIL decided in 1994. Also the Prime Minister told the FICCI annual gathering in 2007 that henceforth Government will only auction such licences. Yet his Minister A. Raja ignored him because he perhaps serves a higher authority.
3. The Union Cabinet resolution of October 31, 2003 had categorically bound future governments to auctioning Telecom licences. This has been flouted by Raja.
4. All the six awardees have subsequently sold the share of their Telecom companies to foreigners at eight time the share value (in terms of paid-up capital per share), thereby proving that they got a bonanza at public cost which made the shares so attractive to buy for foreign companies.
5. None of the Telecom companies have any experience in the field. They received the licence using strong arm methods and goons to muscle into Sanchar Bhavan, New Delhi to come first in the queue physically.
6. But these companies had inter-locking shares in other Telecom companies, which disqualifies them under Clause 8 of the Guidelines mentioned above.
7. The BSNL was not supposed to have any roaming agreement with any operator. But this was violated by allowing the Swan Telecom to have a roaming agreement with BSNL.

The Chief Vigilance Commissioner vide letter dated November 15, 2008 had issued a Show Cause Notice to Telecom Minister A. Raja, who had allotted new licences in 2G mobile services on a "first come, first served" basis to two novice telecom companies, Swan and Unitech. *His move is a complete violation of Clause 8 of the Guidelines for United Access Services Licence issued by the Ministry of Communication and Information Technology Development of Telecommunication,* Government of India {No.lO-21/2005-BS.I(Vol.IT)/49, dated December 14, 2005}, thus causing a loss of over Rs. 50,000 crores to the Government, and consequently according pecuniary benefit to others illegally.

Clause 8 has been violated as follows: While Anil Dhirubhai Ambani Group (ADAG), the promoters of Reliance Communications (R Corn), had more than 10 per cent stake in Swan Telecom, the figures were manipulated and showed as 9,99 per cent holding to beat the said Clause. The documents available disclose that on March 2, 2007, when Swan Telecom applied for United Access Services Licences, it was owned 100 per cent by Reliance Communications and its associates viz. Reliance Telecom, and by Tiger Trustees Limited, Swan Infonet Services Private Limited, and Swan Advisory Services Private Limited (see Annexure 1). At one or the other point of time, employees of ADAG (Himanshu Agarwal, Ashish Karyekar, Paresh Rathod) or its associate companies have been acquiring the shares of Swan Telecom itself. But still the ADAG manipulated the holdings in Swan to reduce it to only 9.99 per cent. Ambani has now quietly sold his shares in Swan to Delphi Investments, a Mauritius based company owned by Ahmed O. Alfl, specializing in automobile spare parts. In turn, Swan has sold 45% of its shares to UAE's Emirates Telecom Corporation (Eti Salat) for Rs. 9000 crores! All these are highly suspicious and not normal business transactions. Swan company got 60% of the 22 Telecom licenced areas at a throw away price of Rs. 1650 crores, when it was worth Rs. 60,000 crores total.

Rcom has operations in the same circles where the application for Swan Telecom was filed. Therefore under Clause 8 of the Guidelines, Swan should not have been allotted spectrum by the Telecommunication Ministry. But the company did get it on

FROM : FAX NO. : 9 Nov. 17 2008 04:15PM P1

सचिव
केन्द्रीय सतर्कता आ
भारत सरकार
SECRETARY
GOVERNMENT OF I
CENTRAL VIGILANCE COM
Satarkta Bhawan, G.P.O. C
Block A, INA, New Delhi 1
Tel. : 011-24618891
Dated 15.11.2008

K.S. RAMASUBBAN

D.O. No. 007/P&T/095-25398

Dear Shri Behura,

Kindly refer to letter No. L-14047/33/2007-NTG(Pt.), dated 15.4.2008, of the Department of Telecom, regarding the reply of the Department on the policy of allocation of spectrum. The Commission has observed that the reply furnished by the Department is neither complete nor specific. Concerns of the Commission and clarifications / information required from the Department, regarding allocation of 2G spectrum and 3G spectrum, are given in the enclosed note.

The Commission has desired that you may personally look into the matter and arrange to send reply to the issues contained in the enclosed note within two weeks.

With Regards, Yours sincerely,

(KS Ramasubban).

Shri Siddhartha Behura,
Secretary,
Department of Telecommunications,
Sanchar Bhawan,
New Delhi- 110 001.

Urgent/. Please process on each and every

Central Vigilance Commission Secretary K.S. Ramasubban's letter to DoT Secretary Siddhartha Behura, dated 15 November 2008

Minister's direction, which is an undue favour from him. There was obviously a *quid pro quo* which only a CBI enquiry can reveal, after an FIR is registered. There is no need for a preliminary enquiry, because the CVC has already done the preliminary enquiry.

It has to be investigated whether two officers of the Department of Telecom—RJS Kushwaha and D. Jha, who were opposed to showing undue favour to Swan Telecom—were transferred just prior to the allotment of the spectrum.

BSNL, which has never done any roaming agreement with any operator, was forced to do a roaming agreement with Swan Telecom, (ironically BSNL does not extend this facility to any other operator). It is quite clear from the agreement that those who are at the helm of affairs of BSNL worked in favour of Swan Telecom. Quite surprisingly, the 2G spectrum licences were priced at 2001 levels to benefit these privateplayers. That was when there were only 4 million cellphone subscribers; now it is 350 million. Hence this simply cannot be 2001 price applicable today.

Immediately after acquiring 2G spectrum licences both Swan and Unitech sold their stakes to foreign companies at a huge profits.

While Swan Telecom sold its stakes to UAE telecom operator Etisalat, Unitech signed a deal with Telenor of Norway for selling its share at huge premiums.

In the process of this 2G spectrum allocation, the government received only one-sixth of what it would have got had it gone through a fresh auction route. The total loss to the exchequer of giving away 2G GSM spectrum in this way—including to the CDMA operators—is over Rs. 50,000 crores and it is said to be one of the biggest financial scams of all times in the country.

While approving the 2G licences, Minister Raja turned a blind eye to the fact that these two companies do not have any infrastructure to launch their services. Falsely claiming that the Telecom Regulatory Authority of India had approved the first-cum-first served rule, Raja went ahead with the 2G spectrum allocation to two debutants in the Telecom sector. In fact earlier TRAI had discussed the spectrum allocation issue with existing services providers and suggested to the Telecom Ministry that spectrum allocation be made through a transparent tender and auction process. This is confirmed by what the TRAI Chairman N. Misra told the CII organized conference on November 28,2008 {Annexure 2}. But Raja did not bother to listen to the TRAI either and pursued the process on "first come, first served" basis, thereby giving a windfall to those who had inside information, and causing a loss of Rs. 50,000 crores to the Government. His dubious move has been to ensure benefit to others at the cost of the national exchequer.

Sources claim that Swan and Unitech not only paid a heavy amount as bribe to the Minister for getting the Spectrum, but also they made every effort to appease senior DoT officials. The Minister and his associates worked in nexus with Swan and Unitech and ensured their smooth sailing in getting spectrum BSNL, which has never done any roaming agreement with any operator, was forced to do a roaming agreement with Swan Telecom. Ironically BSNL does not extend this facility to any other operator. It is quite clear from the agreement that those who are at the helm of affairs of BSNL worked in favour of Swan Telecom.

Quite surprisingly, the 2G spectrum licences were priced at 2001 levels to benefit these private players. Immediately after acquiring 2G spectrum licences both Swan and Unitech sold their stakes to foreign companies at a huge profits: While Swan Telecom sold its stakes to UAE telecom operator Etisalat, Unitech signed a deal with Telenor of Norway for selling its share at huge premiums.

Not only did a commercial organisation, with the Minister's wife as a director, begin operating from his official residence, well-placed sources said the information was concealed from the Prime Minister in violation of Service Rules. The Minister did not also deem it necessary to file an affidavit of 'non-conflict of interest' between his family's business activities and his role as a Union Minister. In course of time, the address was changed and his wife officially withdrew from the firm. But the company's association with the Raja family continued as closely as before, with the shares distributed among his kith and kin.

Green House Promoters Private Limited was formed barely four months after Raja became a Cabinet Minister (in charge of Environment and Forests) for the first time in May 2004. The Chennai-based real estate company was floated with an initial capital of only Rs 1 lakh, with AM Sadhick Batcha—a close associate of Raja—as managing director and Sadhick's wife Reha Banu as a director. Sadhick hails from the Minister's Perambalur constituency in Tamil Nadu. Documents filed with the Registrar of Companies show that Raja's close relatives—such as his brother, nephew, niece and a few others—subsequently became directors in the company. With these high-profile inductions, the share capital of the firm surged to a respectable Rs. 3 crore within 14 months of the operations being launched.

Three years later, in February 2007, the Minister's wife, MA Parameswari, was added to the board as a director. Raja neither informed the Prime Minister of his wife's and other relatives' business activities, which he was required to do according to the Services (Conduct) Rules, nor did he file an affidavit assuring that there would not be a conflict of interest between his duties as a Minister and the business deals of his wife and other relatives.

Even as Green House Promoters Private Limited continued to expand its real estate activities in Tamil Nadu (and Karnataka), with the Minister's official residence doubling up as his wife's business address, Raja was jolted by a report in early 2008 in a section of the media that pulled up the then Union Home Minister Shivraj Patil for using his official address as the business address for his son. Sensing trouble ahead, Raja got into damage control mode. His wife resigned from the directorship of the company on February 2008, but not before transferring her shares to another relative.

Documents available with *The Pioneer* show the shares were transferred to Raja's niece, Malarvizhi. The 29-year-old is the wife of Raja's nephew, a Government pleader in Tamil Nadu. The joint managing director of Green House is Raja's elder nephew RP Paramesh Kumar. The Minister's brother, A Kaliaperumal, is also a director of Green House. Another director of this company is R. Ram Ganesh, the 22-year-old son of Raja's elder brother A. Ramchandran, who is an Indian Forest Service officer.

From a humble beginning of Rs 1 lakh, the company soon soared to great heights. One of the Green House company's accounts at Canara Bank's T. Nagar branch in Chennai has had remittances of more than Rs. 150 crore over the last four years. The money came from the Middle East, Hong Kong and Singapore, besides India, though it remains unclear why these remittances were made.

As the volume of business transactions increased, the company opened an office in Singapore in 2006. According to sources, it was done to cut down on the direct flow of funds into its Indian accounts and thus escape public scrutiny.

The failure to inform the Prime Minister and file an affidavit was not a one-time lapse or an "oversight" by Raja. Wife Parameswari and the Minister's relatives became active partners in another company floated a month after Green House came into existance. Breaching rules again, Raja did not inform the Prime Minister and filed no affidavit of non-conflict of interest. The new company, once again dealing in real estate, had a miraculously high turnover of Rs. 755 crore in its very first year of operation.

When the spectrum controversy began to spin out of control and Telecom Minister A. Raja was recently censured in the media and by political leaders for his questionable decisions, his leader, M. Karunanidhi condemned the critics as people who could "not tolerate the rise of a humble Dalit." The "humble Dalit" of course had allowed his ministerial clout and official address to be used for business, which later connected with the spectrum deal, is now under the scanner of the High Court and the Central Vigilance Commission (CVC). This is a new definition of immunity that Karunanidhi seeks.

The question remains: Why the Board of Directors failed in ensuring good governance of Satyam and Spectrum? As Pratip Kar, a former Director of SEBI, and currently with the Global Corporate Governance Forum of the IFC, Washington D.C., has pointed out (in "Patterns in Governance Failure" *Business Standard* April 13, 2009), a Board of Directors of company cannot be relised as of now to monitor cooperation since it is usually packed with persons of repute bringing a measure of respectability to the company behind which it hides comfortably from serious scrutiny till it is too late. Reputable auditors also enhance the respectability. (For example, Arthur Anderson was Enron's auditor; Grant Thornton was Parmalat's auditor; Enron had a Board and a Audit Committee whose members were the envy of corporate America, just as Satyam had well-respected academicians from Harvard Business School and technology experts in its Board).

The objective of the company shifts to rapid growth and quick rise in profitability in a period of high leveraged-growth under the facile assumption of availability of unlimited liquidity at all times, engineered by leveraging and complex derivatives such as securitized mortages and CDS etc. For example, Enron changed its business from being a energy producer to a derivative trader; Robert Maxwell grew through highly leveraged acquisitions in a short span of 10 years, the celebrated Denis Kozlowski of Tyco Global, made 1,000 acquisitions between 1992 and 2001) by such financial products and derivatives.

At one point of time, the support of the political infrastructure and knowing people in high places becomes important (Calisto Tanzi courted politicians, bankers, bureaucrats; Ken Lay was close friend of the First Family of the US; Robert Maxwell was a long-time member of U.K.'s Labour Party; political circles in Andhra Pradesh were always at home to Ramalinga Raju). There follows a period of extraordinary business success of the company, and the company and those behind it win plaudits and accolades (Enron became one of America's most admired companies; Satyam Computers won awards in corporate governance). There is an air of arrogance and smugness within the company. The persons become the acknowledged gurus of management (Jeff Skilling, Robert Maxwell, Bernie Ebbeers, Ramalinga Raju). This is also the period of high philanthropy as Kar notes, of Beluga caviar and Moet and Chandon parties, of high life and Armani suits and buying up football clubs and FI participation (like Tanzi). A selected few know the truth about numbers but they collude and conspire in silence. There is however uneasiness in the staff in the company, but the source of that anxiety cannot be traced.

Table: Selected cases of corporate fraud

Company	Year	Audit firm	Company	Notes
Nugan Hand Bank	1980	PW	Australia	Money laundering; organized crime
ZZZZ Best	1986	Ernst & Whinney	USA	Barry Minkow; went bust in 1987
MiniScribe	1989	Coopers & Lybrand	USA	Falsifying receivables Numbers to increase Sales, beat the market
Robert Maxwell	1991	Coopers & Lybrand	UK	do
BCCI	1991	PW; E&Y	UK	Fraud and corruption; Underworld

Barings Bank	1995	Deloitte & Touch & Coopers & Lybrand	UK	Fruad
Computer Associates	2000	KPMG	USA	Sanjay Kumar
Xerox	2000	KPMG	USA	Falsifying financia Results
Enron	2001	Arthur Andersen	USA	Jeff Skilling, Ken Lay Andrew Fastow
Adelphia	2002	Deloitte	USA	John Rigas
Bristol-Myers Squibb	2002	PW	USA	Inflated revenues
Dynegy	2002	Deloitte	USA	John Rigas
Bristol-Myers Squibb	2002	PW	USA	Inflated revenues
Dynegy	2002	Arthur Anderson	USA	Round trip trades
El Pasco Corporation	2002	Deloitte	USA	Round trip trades
Freddie	Mac	2002	USA	Understated earnings
Global Crossing	2002	Arthur Anderson	USA	Network capacity Swaps to inflate Revenues
Kmart	2002	PW	USA	Misleading Accounting Practices
Qwest Communications	2002	Arthur Anderson	USA	Inflated revenues
Tyco International	2002	PW	Bermuda	Improper accounting, Dennis Kozlowski
WorldCom	2002	Arthur Anderson	USA	Overstated cash flows Bernard Ebbers
Pamalat	2003	G&T	Italy	Falsified accounting Papers, Calisto Tanzi
Satyam Computer Services	2009	PW	India	Falsified accounts

Source: Kar, Pratap: "Pattern of Governance Failure" *Business Standard,* New Delhi, 13/4/09.

But financial numbers need to be good in the eyes of the external world, so those who verify the numbers need to be befriended and given incentives to keep the show going (Calisto Tanzi got Grant Thornton to certify a fakes 4.5 mn account in the Bank of America for 10 years; Arthur Anderson certified all the transactions of Enron in the SPVs; Price Waterhouse certified non-existent cash in Satyam's balance sheet). In this period of joy, the Board also basks in the glory of media hype; the independent directors are happy to come to all expenses paid meetings hoping the company can do no wrong. So they forget to ask the right question or ask why because nobody dared ask "a stupid" question in case they looked silly in front of everyone else. The Board functions, audit committee meetings are dutifully held, the remuneration committee meets and gives high bonuses as rewards for good work. God is propiated and all is well with the world, or so it seems.

The suddenly the Law of Karma strikes—one day there is an external economic shock (Robert Maxwell ran into problems because banks in UK in the late eighties were under pressure and had to recall the loans; there was a Dot.Com bubble burst in 2000, before the Enron collapse). The state of disequilibrium due to high leverage or paper profit or absence of cash in business due to funds diversion, can no long be hidden; truth thus prevails and then all hell breaks loose. The obvious moorings of governance—the Board, audit committees, financial numbers—are washed away. Like cancer there is little time left between detection and death (Enron was finished in 23 weeks; Barings collapsed in 6 weeks; Satyam did not take more than 15 days). The epilogue is that government and regulators pull out all the stops to search and finds scapegoats who can take their share of the blame. That is how corporate fraud occurs in the best of companies again and again. The core truth is that the Emperor wore no clothes, but no adult dared to say what a guileless child obviously could.

Chapter V

Conclusions: What is Still Sundaram in India?

There is a Law of Diminishing Interest operating in India with respect to corruption. There was a time when exposures of even minor cases of corruption e.g., Mundhra and Dharma Teja used to be topics of debate in Parliament, the media and other public forums. But now, issues of corruption and misconduct of politicians and public servants have largely *gone out of public debate.* It is not that corruption has come down. From all *available indications, it has only increased over time.* Are society and media suffering from the Law of Diminishing Interest—i.e., as the magnitude and frequency of corruption rises, public interest in wanting to book the culprits declines?

Is this apathy because corruption has been accepted as a normal fact of public life and there is a feeling that an exposure does not help improve the situation at all? In the 1950s and through the 1960s and right upto the 1980s, society and media were perhaps more alert to public misconduct, judging from the coverage that cases like the Kairon, Nagarwala and Bofors scandals received. The media tried to breach the wall of cynicism by the increasingly direct and sensational methods of exposure it deployed such as sting operations since the 1990s. It was perhaps felt that stronger tools and techniques were needed to shake people out of a sense of resignation. The natural culmination of this process was the use of the sting operation of the current decade, in which corruption or misconduct was caught live and presented directly to the public. It seemed that theatricality was needed to make a greater impact. But this trend too seems to have hit the Law of Diminishing Interest.

There is a corresponding change in the attitudes of the corrupt, or those facing charges of corruption. If there was, in the past, embarrassment, defensiveness or even a readiness to quit office when faced with charges of corruption or misconduct, there is now a brazen nonchalance and sometimes even an aggressive so-what? Witness Sonia Gandhi is utter non-chalance to the expose of her false educational qualification and the Quattrocchi's escape. The posture now is that a sign of confidence (arrogance?) coming from the awareness of greater social acceptance of, or at least less resistance to, corruption in public life.

It may be noted that this perceived change in the attitude to corruption almost coincides with the country's period of economic liberalization. This period, starting in the early 1990s, saw a de-emphasis of the role of the state in social and economic life and greater importance for the private sector, and by implication, the individual. In politics, this was also the period when the party system—the political equivalent of a regulating state—came under pressure and almost broke down, and the individual leader became more important than the party. It can be suggested that the rising tide of a wrong kind of individualism may have influenced social attitudes to corruption. The argument may thus be posed like this: if corruption is broadly the misuse of public office or assets for private gain, has the identification of the state with the public realm, and the individual with the private realm resulted in a moral confusion and a view of illegal gains and misappropriation of public assets as a "rightful" individual prerogative, especially for the increasingly assertive middle class?

There used to be the notion that corruption is a by product of the controlled economy and its "licence-permit raj." But we find that corruption may have actually grown in scale and scope after controls were loosened. Is it because the individualism that gained strength in this period and is still growing was centred around an idea of the individual who grows at society's expense and who has little commitment to society? Importantly, the historical circumstances that helped the rise and growth of individualism elsewhere were not available in India. Did the media take its cue from this change in the idea of the individual and his/her relationship with society? Does its keenness to appeal to an indifferent society and self-indulgent individual, explain the diminishing concern about corruption and even the rise of the sensationalist and Page 3 cultures?

But for India there is still hope. Despite waves and waves of foreign marauders, loot and debasement, the civilization of India is a unbroken continuing one in which high thinking and simple living is still a moral value. The 20th century national heroes were Mahatma Gandhi and Jayaprakash Narayan, revered for their symbolizing this moral value. Sacrifice and service is still the most elevated attributes that people want in their leaders. What is required therefore is the assertion of the silent majority of Indians to enforce probity and restrain greed. That is the "Sundaram" still surviving in 21st century India.

INDEX